Leasing Away a Nation

The Legacy of Catawba Indian Land Leases

By Louise Pettus

On the front: A young member of the Catawba Nation performs a tribal dance during the Catawbas' annual Yap Ye Iswa Festival. Photo courtesy of The Herald / Travis Bell

Dear Friends:

Founders Federal Credit Union is proud to sponsor Leasing Away a Nation by Louise Pettus. The story of this key aspect in the development of the South Carolina Piedmont is well worth telling.

For over fifty years Founders Federal Credit Union has helped our communities reach their potential by giving our citizens the resources to reach their goals. The mission of Founders includes promoting the appreciation of our unique history as key to understanding the future of our area. Ms. Pettus' book is a fine publication for heightening this understanding.

We are also pleased to be partners in this project with three outstanding non-profit organizations. Katawba Valley Land Trust, Nation Ford Land Trust and Palmetto Conservation Foundation all make invaluable contributions to our quality of life and we salute their efforts.

Louise Pettus has added greatly to our knowledge about the founding of our area through this wonderful book. She has always demonstrated a special understanding our history and we are pleased to make her work available to our friends and neighbors.

Founders Federal Credit Union hopes you enjoy Leasing Away a Nation.

Bruce Brumfield
President and CEO
Founders Federal Credit Union

Palmetto Conservation Foundation appreciates the support of Congressman John Spratt and the Close/Springs Foundation in the development of this book.

Edited by Cal Harrison.
Design and layout by Susan Jones Ferguson.

Published by Palmetto Conservation Foundation/PCF Press PO Box 1984, Spartanburg, SC 29304. www.palmettoconservation.org

10 09 08 07 06 05 04 03 02 01

A c k n o w l e d g m e n t s

I don't think I would have, or could have, compiled this book without the Surveyor's Plat Book and Indian Commissioners' Rent Book, which was preserved by Hugh M. White of Fort Mill, a descendant of Hugh Monroe White, who kept the book from 1811 to 1840. In the course of writing this book, Mr. White graciously agreed to allow me to take the only surviving commissioners' book to the state Department of Archives and History to be photographed and microfilmed. Nor would this book have ever been completed without the assistance and encouragement of my brother, D. Lindsay Pettus. Especially helpful also were Robert Mackintosh of the State Archives staff and my housemate, Martha D. Bishop, who tolerated the piles of paper that accompanied the search. I was also encouraged by Congressman John M. Spratt who once remarked to me that if I did not write this book, no one else would. I deeply appreciate his willingness to write the foreword.

Louise Pettus
2005

The Katawba Valley Land Trust is a nonprofit, private conservation organization dedicated to the protection of natural resources, open lands, waters, historic resources, and vistas of aesthetic value in the Catawba River Valley and surrounding areas of South Carolina.

The Nation Ford Land Trust is a nonprofit, private conservation organization dedicated to the enhancement of the quality of life of the York County area by preserving its open spaces, natural beauty, and scenic heritage.

The Palmetto Conservation Foundation is a statewide nonprofit membership organization based in Columbia and with offices in Spartanburg and Moncks Corner. PCF provides technical assistance on sustainable development, conserves natural and cultural resources, and promotes active living. Learn more at www.palmettoconservation.org

Built on the west bank of the Catawba River in 1830, Garrison's Mill was destroyed by the Great Flood of 1916. Print courtesy of Jack Bolin, 1977

Table of Contents

Foreword

When Louise Pettus first told me that she was considering this study, I encouraged her to pursue it. I knew that the sources were arcane, but I also knew that Louise Pettus had a command of the subject and that no one could do the study or tell the story better. What she produced is what I expected—diligent scholarship and readable history.

This is the story of how the Catawbas acquired 225 square miles of land and then leased away most of it. It is a small but important slice of American history. The European settlers of North America were land-hungry; yet the means by which they acquired land are hardly told in American history. As white settlers moved over the continent, they encountered native Americans who possessed or laid claim to large tracts of land. For more than a century, Indian land was a bloody bone of contention, but a struggle seldom told in any depth. I studied history but never learned anything of aboriginal or Indian title or of the Indian Non-Intercourse Act of 1790. I am an avid reader of South Carolina history, but until the Catawbas asserted their claim to 140,000 acres, I knew little about the Treaty of Augusta. I knew something of the Snow Campaign against the Cherokee, but little about how land tenure was an underlying cause. Louise Pettus fills part of that void and makes clear why all students of the period should pay closer attention to these matters.

This is a worthy work for many reasons, but first because it is well-founded local history. Local history tends to be long on legend and embellished as it is handed down. Louise Pettus writes fluently and tells a good story, but she sticks to the sources, which makes her work authoritative.

At the heart of this study is an aboriginal people who came to be known as the Catawbas. Like much native American history, theirs is tragic. In the early 1700s when they were identified by an English botanist named John Lawson, the Catawbas were a small but proud tribe, living along the banks of the river, which bears their name. They took the side of the English in the war with France, and in 1760 were awarded by the Treaty of Pine Tree Hill a tract of 144,000 acres or 225 square miles. This grant was confirmed by the Treaty of Augusta in 1763, and Samuel Wylie, a partner of Joseph Kershaw, was commissioned to survey the boundaries, fifteen miles on each side. Wylie's survey was completed in 1764 at a time when the Catawbas were suffering the third epidemic of smallpox to strike their people during the 1700s. This bout decimated their tribe, and left them easy prey to white settlers seeking land.

My forebear, Thomas Spratt, apparently settled on the lands set aside to the Catawbas before or shortly after the Treaty of Augusta, but during most of the Revolutionary War, Catawba land was no-man's land to white settlers. This is why the New Acquisition militia mustered here in 1780 and chose Thomas Sumter as their commander shortly after the fall of Charleston. According to a contemporary account by David Hutchison, many of the young men who served with Sumter found themselves "poor and penniless" after the war and were "encouraged by the Indians and whites already settled to come and live on their land."

The leasing of Catawba land was soon underway in earnest. Leases are said to have been signed for all sorts of inducement, a good saddle or a fine musket, but usually for nominal rent. In 1785, the state formalized the practice by requiring leases to be written and signed by leaders of the tribe. The state also appointed local commissioners to oversee the process, and required their "approbation" to validate a lease. Instead of protecting the Catawbas, these steps had the effect of sanctioning the leases, and in the words of Louise Pettus: "The market for wholesale leasing of the Catawbas' land was open, and over the next fifty-six years, it would become big business."

The intrusion of white settlers was by no means unique to the Catawbas. White settlers encroached on the lands of native Americans from Maine to Georgia. Some took title by purchase and deed, some by lease, some by squatting and laying claim to adverse possession. Dishonest dealings were all too common, and often resulted in violence. To pacify the frontier, the British barred white settlements in Indian land. The Congress of the United States followed the same policy. In 1790, at the request of President Washington, Congress enacted the first Indian Non-Intercourse Act, a law prohibiting white settlers or states from acquiring Indian land unless the transaction was ratified by Congress.

Among the Indian tribes traveling to Philadelphia to petition Congress with their grievances were the Catawbas. This was the first of many pleas they would bring to the federal government, only to be rebuffed, or in this case, referred to the state of South Carolina for redress.

In the early 1800s, as the Catawbas grew more apprehensive about the loss of their land, the settlers became anxious about their leaseholds. They worried about the longevity of their leases and reports of Lowcountry landowners angling to acquire the Catawbas' reversionary interest. The leaseholders pressed the state for protection, and in 1840 their efforts finally bore fruit. The leadership of a much-diminished tribe signed the Treaty of Nation Ford with the state of South Carolina, ceding title to 144,000 acres. The state granted the leaseholders fee simple title in return for their commitment to pay assessments to fund the $21,000 in cash promised the Catawbas. The state also promised the Catawbas to buy land in Haywood County, North Carolina where they could relocate and live with the Cherokee, a plan that was dropped when the Governor of North Carolina protested. In lieu of a tract in North Carolina, 630 acres of red clay land were carved out of the Catawbas' old domain and conveyed to the tribe.

The Catawba Tribe dwindled almost to the vanishing point, but remnant members did not forget the Treaty of 1840. They spent the next century trying to right this wrong.

By the 1940s, the federal government occupied a position of trust over the Catawbas, but offered no help in enforcing the tribe's claim, and in fact, allowed the claim to be eroded away by time without ever warning the Catawbas of the consequences. Ironically, the tribe's restoration resulted from a boundary dispute involving the Passamaquoddy in Maine. An elderly Passamaquoddy woman produced a box of papers she had kept for years under her bed. These papers came to the attention of an intern named Tom Tureen. He took the documents, and months later informed the incredulous Indians that they held claim to much of the state of Maine. Their lands had been ceded by a treaty that was never ratified under the Indian Non-Intercourse Act. Tureen's analysis was borne out when the First Circuit Court of Appeals held that the Indian Non-Intercourse Act applied to eastern Indian land claims, and was not subject to any statute of limitations or repose.

After the federal courts' decision in the Penobscot and Passamaquoddy case, the Catawba claim took on fresh validity, but the federal government again declined to help. The Catawbas at long last turned to the Native American Rights Fund (NARF), and to another young lawyer named Don Miller, who would spend almost twenty years advocating their case before prevailing. Those who think that our society is too litigious and that class action suits are an abuse should read this account. Justice was finally rendered in the Catawba case only because NARF had mastered the law of Indian claims, and was ready, willing, and allowed to sue.

I followed the Catawba case closely from the time their claim was first asserted, and spent a good part of four years helping to hammer out a settlement and then sell it to federal, state, and local governments. Its enactment was one of my most satisfying accomplishments in Congress, one that I believe Thomas "Kanawha" Spratt would have approved.

Pieces of the Catawbas' story have been told before, but Louise Pettus stitches them together with an easily flowing narrative that combines the right amounts of information and indignation, and reveals her mastery of the material. To this narrative Louise Pettus adds a wealth of detail about Catawba Indian leases that has never been assembled. Whether you are interested in American history, native American history, genealogy, or local land acquisition, this book is worth reading, studying, and having on your shelf. We are indebted to Louise Pettus for tireless scholarship and a valuable work of history.

John M. Spratt Jr.
2005

Introduction

In 1973, when I read *The Catawba Indians, The People of the River* by Douglas Summers Brown, I was surprised to learn on page 295 that one of my ancestors was once turned away by the South Carolina Legislature:

"In the year 1808, William Pettus, a lessee of the Indian Land, a duly elected representative, was sent home by the Legislature, which refused to seat him. He was not recognized on the ground that he was not a free holder. This was the first indication to the white settlers within the Indian Boundary that, although they were subject to taxes and other responsibilities as citizens, they were without representation in the government under which they lived. This discovery led to the enactment of full legislation by the State of South Carolina on the subject of the Catawba Indian lands and those who occupied it."

I wanted to learn more about the people and events of this era. Who were the original white settlers? Who were their Catawba landlords? What sort of lease agreements did they make?

Many South Carolina history books discuss the importance of two major milestones—the Treaty of Augusta in 1763 and the Treaty of Nation Ford in 1840. Surprisingly little has been written about the seventy-seven years between those two treaties.

The leaseholding era began shortly after the signing of the Treaty of Augusta, in which the royal governor of South Carolina awarded the Catawba Indian tribe a 225-square-mile reservation in central Carolina on both sides of the Catawba River at the intersection of two major trading routes. In a practice that was unique among American Indian tribes, the Catawbas allowed individual tribal members to rent their land to white settlers for terms of up to ninety-nine years.

From the beginning, the state-sanctioned leasing system was fraught with problems—squatters who refused to pay rent and neighbors who engaged in heated boundary disputes. The tribal Head Men grew dissatisfied with the Indian commissioners, and the leaseholders repeatedly complained about living in a no-man's land, lacking state representation and clear title to their land. The Catawbas were unhappy with the rent payments, and the leaseholders were increasingly resentful of their landlords.

As I reviewed the historical documents of the leaseholder period, in my mind's eye, I began to see Catawba Indian Land as a diamond-shaped mosaic. Within this mosaic were hundreds of survey plats, like irregular tiles bordered by creeks and roads that are familiar landmarks. In the beginning, there was plenty of empty space, but over the years I filled it in one plat at a time—red tiles for the Catawbas and white tiles for the white settlers. Red dominated the mosaic at the outset of the leaseholder era, but as time went on, red tiles were replaced with white tiles. Within two generations, the white tiles were dominant. By 1840, only a few dots of red remained.

Attaching names to this mosaic was not easy. The task required many trips to the South Carolina Department of Archives and History, which houses 128 of the original leases and many related papers. I could locate only one of the three Indian commissioners' books, which contain copies of the surveyor's plats and rent records. I spent many hours reading the Surveyor's Plat Book and Indian Commissioners' Rent Book, which contains records for the east side of the Catawba River from 1811 to 1840. [1] I found records of more than 1,300 leases and subleases, which were bought, sold and passed down to children and grandchildren.

The commissioners' book came to an abrupt end in 1840 with the Treaty of Nation Ford. Under the treaty, the Catawbas traded away all rights to the reservation for $21,000 in cash payments and land in the mountains of North Carolina. In exchange, the leaseholders received land grants and clear title to most of present-day Fort Mill and Rock Hill, and Indian Land in Lancaster County.

As history has shown, the tribe's claim to its 144,000-acre reservation was far from settled. For seventy-seven years, the Catawbas and the settlers had embarked on a grand experiment in land development that failed miserably. The Treaty of Augusta said nothing about the Indians renting the land. There was nothing to guide the Catawbas in their role as landlord, nor was there a single word to restrain or instruct white men eager to become leaseholders. In retrospect, it is amazing that the two groups of vastly different cultures got along as well as they did.

Problems that plagued the leaseholder period and the failure of state and federal government to intervene were sources of bitterness for the Catawbas passed down through the next five generations. Eventually, mistakes made by South Carolina in the 1800s would resurface in the form of a federal land claim lawsuit filed in 1980. Before the lawsuit was settled for $50 million in 1993, the Catawbas' land claim cast a shadow over titles held by 62,000 York and Lancaster County landowners— many of them descendants of the area's original leaseholders.

What follows is the story of the land, the landlords and the leaseholders and what the historical record tells us about their interactions.

Louise Pettus
2005

1) No one knows what happened to the first book, which was kept by Charles Miller from 1785 to 1809. The third book, which contained records for the west side of the river, is believed to have been lost in the 1850s in a fire that destroyed Josina Garrison's house in Ebenezer.

Chapter One

The Land

"The chief settlement of the Katahbas is contiguous to Charlestown in South Carolina and as near as I can compute it from frequent journeys, is about two hundred miles distant. The Katahbas are settled close on the east side of a broad, purling river that heads in the great Blue Ridge of mountains and empties itself into the Santee river."

- James Adair, 1743.

It is easy to see today why the Catawbas' land would be so valuable to the Carolinas. Located on the outskirts of Charlotte, North Carolina, the land is bisected by the Catawba River and situated along a major transportation corridor, Interstate 77. The area's first explorers also saw it as highly desirable land, and for many of the same reasons.

Turn your thoughts back over three centuries ago. A young Englishman in his twenties by the name of John Lawson had just landed at the port of Charles Town in 1701. In his pocket he carried a commission from the Crown to be the first Surveyor General of North Carolina. Lawson was not trained to be a surveyor. A college graduate with a special interest in botany, he had wrangled the appointment to get free passage to pursue his hobby. European scientists of his day believed the discovery of new plants in the New World would lead to cures for diseases that had plagued the Old World for centuries. Lawson and other botanists believed the roots, berries, or bark of these plants would have special healing qualities. Lawson never found those miraculous plants, but his travels across the Carolinas yielded important discoveries about the land and the tribal people who inhabited it.

Lawson hired Indian guides and headed upstream along the Ashley River, intending to follow it into North Carolina. From the Ashley River he followed the Santee, then the Congaree and Wateree until reaching the Catawba River at present-day Camden. All along the way he stopped at Indian villages, spaced about ten miles apart. During his visit to the Catawba villages, he wrote that he saw a seven-mile-long field of corn interspersed with beans and peas.[2]

Lawson was referring to the famous Kings Bottoms—a stretch of very fertile

◄ Over the centuries, the Catawba River has served as a boundary between Indian tribes and a vital resource for food, trade, and transportation. Photo courtesy The Herald / Andy Burriss

2) James Adair, who lived among the Catawbas, wrote that there were three varieties of Indian corn: an early variety that ripened in two months; a hominy corn, described as "yellow and flinty," and a white soft-grained corn termed "bread corn."

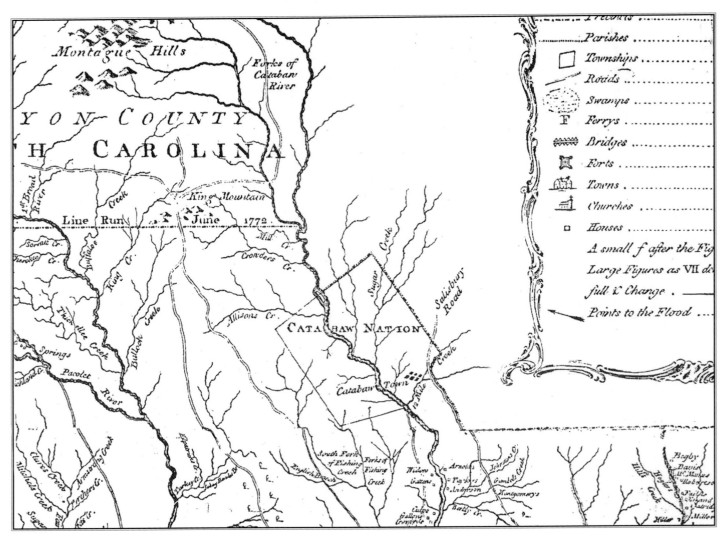

Montague Hills

Forks of Cataban River

...YON COUNTY

...H CAROLINA

Montague Hills

1st Broad River

Sorrell Cr.

Turokee Cr.

Creek

King Cr.

Buffaloe Cr.

Line Run

King Mountain

June 1772

Mill Cr.

Cronders Cr.

Allisons Cr.

Sugar Creek

Salisbury Road

CATABAW NATION

Bullock Creek

Thickittee Creek

Springs

Pacolet

Richland Cr.

Pacolet River

Fanning Creek

Catabaw Town

½ Mile

Cr.

Clarks Creek

Mitchells Creek

N. Bobby Cr.

Panthers Cr.

Turkey Cr.

Tinkey Hanks Br.

South Fork of Fishing Creek

English Branch

Forks of Fishing Creek

Wilsons Gattens

Arnolds

Tinkers

Anderson

Johnsons Creek

Cronlds Cr.

Montgomerys

Culps Gallons Crossley's

Baits Cr.

Sugar Br.

Hills Cr.

Heylers Creek

Begby

Davis

McMahos

Roberson

Wylie

Wigand

David

Miller

Miller

Legend:

Precincts ....

Parishes ....

□ Townships ....

Roads ....

Swamps ....

F Ferrys ....

Bridges ....

Forts ....

Towns ....

Churches ....

□ Houses ....

A small f after the Fig...

Large Figures as VII do...

full £ Change ....

Points to the Flood ....

This map, copied by Library of Congress from the original in the British Museum, shows the state boundary in 1772, the tribe's 225-square-mile reservation, and the location of a village called "Catabaw Town". Map Courtesy of Library of Congress

soil in the Indian Land section of Lancaster County. Frequent flooding of the river kept the river bottoms rich with nutrients. The Kings Bottoms stretched from the confluence of Sugar Creek and the Catawba River to Twelve Mile Creek, which is on the north side of the present-day village of Van Wyck. Along the banks of this rich bottomland, the Catawba potters found their favored clay.

Catawba pottery has distinctive mottled colors of black, slate, gray, cream, tan, and orange that vary depending upon the amount of mica and iron oxide in the clay. Catawba potters who still practice the craft today achieve varying effects by firing the ware in an open pit or smothering it with wood chips or sawdust.

Generations of Catawbas had created a vast prairie in present-day York County, using the slash-and-burn method to rid the area of trees and allow grasses to grow. The land was ideal for hunting game, and it was attractive farmland. The first white settlers found miles and miles of grassland with pea vines that grew waist high and cane-brakes along the creeks. There were a few buffalo, a vast number of deer and smaller animals, and many varieties of birds. Flocks of Carolina parakeets and pigeons were so numerous that sometimes when they roosted the tree limbs broke from their weight.

One of the most interesting descriptions of the land comes from Lord Cornwallis, the British general, during the Revolutionary War. Cornwallis had marched into Charlotte where the Waxhaws men, led by Colonel William Richardson Davie, had so harassed him that he called the town a hornet's nest. Cornwallis retreated to the Fort Mill area and in his daybook wrote that the countryside looked like an English park. He noted splendid hardwood forests, chiefly oak and hickory, "with no underbrush but greensward as far as the eye can reach." This park-like atmosphere, Lord Cornwallis said, "alternates with level green prairies with buffalo and deer pasturing over them and an abundance of wild turkey racing through open woods." That was seventy-eight years after John Lawson made his journey.

A half-century later, the state of South Carolina and its districts were surveyed for the first time, and the maps were included

Catawba pottery has remained relatively unchanged for centuries Courtesy of The Herald/Andy Burriss

Sugar Trees Along The Catawba

Compiled in the 1820s. Robert Mills' atlas of South Carolina included a map of each district and a narrative about the landscape. The unknown author of the York narrative wrote that most of the trees were oak, poplar, hickory, and chestnut—with a few short-leaf pine. An even wider variety of trees grew along the Catawba River including sycamore, sassafras, dogwood, ironwood, hackberry, walnut, buckeye, horse chestnut, redbud, cucumber tree, magnolia, paupau and sugar trees.

One sycamore tree measured twenty-eight feet around and nine feet in diameter, while one sugar tree measured ten feet around, or three feet in diameter. According to the author, the sugar tree "has been many times tapped and sugar formerly made from the juice."

in Robert Mills' atlas. Mills traveled extensively throughout South Carolina, and in other writing said there was "in this entire state no place more pleasing than the banks of the Catawba River."

After the arrival of Scots-Irish settlers, the land began to change as these newcomers brought traditional settlement, livestock and cultural practices to the New World.

New settlements that sprouted across the region were based on clachan farms of northern Ireland, which had been transplanted from Scotland:

"Clachans were clusters of related farm families that communally worked a piece of ground. They continuously cultivated the best lands, or infields, maintaining soil fertility by manuring. On the poorer lands or outfields, they practiced shifting cultivation, cropping temporary fields that were returned to fallow pasture when yields declined. Beyond the outfields lay the unclaimed wastes that served as common grazing land for livestock." [3]

The Scots-Irish settlements of York County only partially resembled the clachans of northern Ireland. The Catawbas' land was much more fertile and the population more sparsely settled than that of northern Ireland. The first settlers, naturally seeking the best land possible, were far more scattered—sometimes homesteads were separated by a mile or more. Scots-Irish newcomers usually traveled south from Virginia or Pennsylvania with kinsmen and tended to settle as near to each other as possible. Neighbors helped each other clear the land, build houses, and harvest crops.

From the earliest days, South Carolina law required fencing of crops to allow animals to graze freely. Bottomlands along the creeks of York and Lancaster counties became a version of infields. The outfields were the forested upland areas that had been cleared for crops. When these lands "wore out," they became pasturelands.

Many early plats have notations such as "old field" with some saying "Indian old field." Occasionally a corner of a survey might be a "lick" or "stony lick." These naturally occurring salt rocks attracted deer and cattle. If there were no natural licks, the farmers put out salt to keep their animals tame.

Because the cattle roamed the countryside, it was important to brand the animals. Nicking the ears in a special pattern was practiced, just as in northern Ireland. Each fall calves were rounded up for branding and culling. The farmers often drove the surplus to market or hired drovers to drive them as far north as Philadelphia.

Transportation was one of the major attributes of the area. Many of the trails blazed by animals and Indians became

3) John Solomon Ott, "Cannon's Point Plantation, 1794-1860: Living Conditions and Status Patterns in the Old South,", The Journal of American History, Vol. 72, No. 2, September 1985 p. 404.
4) York Co. Deeds, Book F, #386, pp. 508-12.
5) The Statutes at Large of South Carolina.

An Industry That Gave Fort Mill its Name

Water power from the Catawba River and its tributaries fueled the first industry in the Catawba Indian Land—grist mills for grinding corn and wheat. The town of Fort Mill owes half of its name to Theodoric Webb's mill, which operated on Steele Creek in the 1780s. On the west side of the river not far from present-day Rock Hill, blacksmith Alexander Faris contracted with the Rev. William Blackstock in 1803 to build a mill dam, grist mill and cotton gin on Half Mile Creek near the old Nation Ford.[4]

River fords and roads were ideal locations for other businesses such as taverns and general stores. Recognizing the growing need for improved roads, the state in 1823 authorized:

"… a new road shall be laid out, opened and kept in repair from the old Nation Ford on the Catawba River, through the land of William E. White to John Springs' mill, crossing Half Mile creek at said mill; thence through the land of Alexander Faires, near his house; thence through the lands of Ticer, Joseph Young, Lemuel Thomason, William Gilmore, Abram Miller, Thomas Campbell, David M'Cance, M'Common, M'Elmoi and Pride to the Chester line, near to a place called White's lower mill." [5]

major trading routes along the Atlantic Coast and west to the Mississippi River. These trails generally followed ridges and crossed streams at natural fords. The Nation Ford on the Catawba River was a part of an Indian trading path that started in Philadelphia, traveled through Richmond, Virginia; Salisbury and Charlotte, North Carolina, and Fort Mill, South Carolina. The trail crossed the Catawba River at Rock Hill east of the current site of the Celanese Acetate LCC plant under the Norfolk and Southern Railway trestle.[6]

Nation Ford Road crossed over present-day Red River Road and then split, with one fork turning south toward Rock Hill's Saluda Street and down to Chester where it entered the town of Chester on another Saluda Street, and continued to the town of Saluda. This southern fork led to Augusta, Georgia and thence to the Mississippi River. The northern fork headed to the town of York and meandered on to Abbeville and thence westward. Another major Indian trail became the Charlotte to Camden Road, or the Great Road to Philadelphia, which led south to Charleston and Savannah, Georgia.

The old river fords were later replaced by a system of ferries franchised by the state. The first ferry on the Catawba River was located between Highway 5 and Highway 9 at York County's Ten Mile Creek not far north of the Chester County line. McClenahan's Ferry was in existence in the 1750s.

The state set the rates that the ferry could charge for individuals, horses, wagons, cattle, sheep, hogs, and other loads. The only exceptions were office holders, clergymen and people going to church on Sunday, who rode for free.

Eventually, bridges would replace the ferries. When you cross a bridge on the Catawba today, you can be certain a ferry once operated at that spot.

The land, the streams, the wildlife, the trails, and the climate combined to make the area highly desirable for settlement. But there was one hitch—it was not possible to get title to the land. The Catawba Indians owned this Piedmont gem—all 225 square miles. Even though the Catawbas loved nothing better than a good trade, they were determined to retain ownership of their land.

John Springs' Twelve-Day River Journey

The river was a cheap but sometimes treacherous mode for transporting cotton to the lower part of the state. Boats had to navigate through the shoals at Land's Ford and then bypass the Great Falls downstream.

In March 1832, John Springs III of Fort Mill described the sixty-mile journey from Fort Mill to Camden as follows:

"Twelve days ago Andrew and myself took water at the Old Nation Ford with 46 bales Cotton and in five Days landed it safe in Camden and sold it for 10 cents, and the Boat on its return is bringing two pair Mill stones for a Mill Wm. E. White and myself are now engaged in erecting at the Ford." [7]

As early as 1804, local farmers petitioned the South Carolina Legislature to open up Sugar Creek for navigation from McAlpine Creek to the Catawba River, but the state's only attempt to build locks and a canal on the Catawba would come in the 1820s at Land's Ford. With the rise of the railroads over the next several decades, canals became obsolete.

6) Archaeologist Rita Kenion insists that Nation Ford was not exactly under the trestle (as several early writers have written) but could be "near."
7) Chester County, (S.C.) Public Library, Local History Room.

Chapter Two

The Landlords

According to Indian legend, at least one hundred years before the first white men arrived in the Carolinas, the Catawbas and Cherokees fought a great battle. The fighting lasted a full day and ended only when both sides were too exhausted to continue. They agreed that neither tribe would occupy the land on the west side of the Catawba River between the Catawba and Broad rivers. In the same manner that tribes in the Ohio Valley designed Kentucky as common hunting land, the Catawbas and the Cherokees agreed to let both tribes hunt in the area of present-day York and Chester counties.

This no-man's land extended from far up in the North Carolina mountains down to the confluence of the two rivers into the Santee River. Thus, the Catawbas kept the richest soil along the Catawba River.

As a result of the treaty with the Cherokees, a series of Catawba Indian villages were established on the east side of the Catawba River. The river was the focal point for the tribe. The Catawbas were first called "Esaws," a corruption of the word "river" in their Siouan language. After his visit in 1700, surveyor John Lawson identified six named villages along the river. The chief village, referred to as Turkeyhead in early land leases, can be easily found today at the site of Roddey Bridge, which spanned the Catawba River prior to the flood of 1916. Although the largest Catawba village was located in Fort Mill Township, most were located in present-day Lancaster County.

This concentration of villages along well-traveled trading routes enabled the Catawbas to become a trading nation. White traders from Charles Town and as far away as Pennsylvania competed for the tribe's business.

By the time the first white families arrived in the Catawba Indian Land in the 1750s, the tribe had been dealing with white traders from Virginia for more than a century and with colonial government officials in Charles Town (later renamed Charleston) since 1680.

From the beginning, Indians and whites each wanted something the other had to offer. White men particularly wanted the Indians' deer and beaver skins, not to mention Indian medicines. Indians were invaluable trackers of both animals and runaway slaves. Knowing their way over Upcountry trails, Catawba Indians were

◄ Eastern Indian garb was simple yet functional, unlike the elaborate head-dresses commonly associated with Western tribes.

often hired as guides or messengers to deliver messages hundreds of miles away for a low cost. In exchange for their services, the Indians wanted guns and ammunition, knives, rum, cloth, and blankets and lesser items such as mirrors, beads, and bracelets.

Most of the trading occurred through a barter system, but by the 1790s money was playing an increasingly important role in tribal life. The South Carolina Council regularly paid Catawbas cash bounties for runaway slaves and Cherokee scalps, and it paid doctors, gunsmiths, and tavern keepers for services rendered to the Catawbas.

The Catawbas were geographically well positioned for trade, and the tribe became known as keen traders and accomplished middlemen between other tribes. Catawba pottery had been traded by Indians for centuries before the arrival of white men, and pottery-making has remained an important part of the tribal economy since the colonial era. A considerable amount of Catawba pottery has been found by archaeologists from Pennsylvania to the Mississippi River. Archaeologists also have observed that as trade with the white men increased over time, the craftsmanship that went into their pots and baskets diminished.

The Catawbas approached trade quite differently from the white traders. The tribe had no written language for recording transactions. Nor did the Catawbas have tools of measurement. For instance, white traders seeking furs carried steelyards with them to weigh the bulky masses of skins. The Indians had no iron implements and were suspicious of scales they could not read.

Still, the Catawbas opened their villages to the visiting traders. It was a custom in Indian society to act as the host to strangers passing through. Traders who graciously accepted the offer of food and lodging and found to be acceptable were offered a wife from the tribe. Many traders married Indian women who served as their interpreters.

In addition to being a trading nation, the Catawbas were a nation of warriors. The British superintendent of Indian Affairs said, "In war, they are inferior to no Indian whatever."[9]

The tribe's bitter conflict with the Cherokees had spanned generations, and when the French and Indian Wars erupted in 1754, it was inevitable that the Catawbas would be asked to serve. In February 1756, the governor of Virginia dispatched a delegation to the Catawbas seeking warriors to fight against the French. The following November, Colonel George Washington reported that eleven Catawbas reported for duty at Winchester, Virginia. Eventually, 124 Catawbas would serve in the army, mostly as scouts for British soldiers.

Historian James Merrell said the size of the tribe was "not very impressive when set alongside the 3,000 Cherokee or the 1,500

'We Expect to Live on Those Lands We Now Possess'

In 1754, few white settlers had moved into the area, but the Catawbas' claim to their ancestral land was spelled out in these excerpts of "King Hagler's Talk," translated by Indian agent Matthew Toole.

"... we Expect to live on those Lands we now possess During our Time here for when the Great man above made us he also made this Island. He also made our forefathers and of this Colour and Hue. He also fixed our forefathers and us here to Inherit this Land and Ever since we Lived after our manner and fashion ..."

The Catawba chief emphasized the tribe's dependence on "the white people" for essential goods, such as knives, axes, scissors and clothing. Hagler pledged his loyalty to the British colonies of South Carolina, North Carolina and Virginia.

"... to this Day we have lived in a Brotherly Love & peace with them and more Especially with these Three Governments, and it is our Earnest Desire that Love and Friendship, which has so Long remain'd should Ever continue."[8]

Creek, but enough to sustain a native society in the piedmont and earn the Catawba Nation a place as one of the four 'most considerable' Indian peoples in the Southeast."[10]

To the British, the Catawbas had long provided somewhat of a buffer against the hostile Cherokees. Their chief, King Hagler,

8) Douglas Summers Brown, The Catawba Indians: The People of the River, University of South Carolina Press, 1953, p. 217.
9) James Merrell, The Indian's New World, University of North Carolina Press, 1989 p. 119.
10) Merrell, p. 17.

boasted, "We are a small Nation, but our Name is high." Above all, the Catawbas were considered staunch allies of the British. Royal Governor James Glen called them "as brave fellows as any on the continent of America and our firm friends."

A major reason for the friendship was King Hagler (also spelled Haggler, Haglar, Hegler, and Heiglar). He has been called the greatest of Catawba leaders, which was certainly the viewpoint of whites who benefited from Hagler's loyalty to the royal governor. Conversely, Hagler depended on the governor to keep the peace with white settlers and enemy tribes—and among the Catawbas.

Hagler's murder in 1763 by a raiding band of Shawnee Indians from Virginia created immediate panic across the frontier. Many of the Scots-Irish settlers had traveled to the Waxhaws to escape the rampages and torchings in Pennsylvania and Virginia during the French and Indian Wars. They thought they were safe among the Catawbas. The loss of Hagler was a severe blow.

King Hagler was killed at the end of the French and Indian Wars, just four months before the Treaty of Augusta. The Catawba warriors had returned from the war and brought smallpox to their villages. Smallpox epidemics in 1700 and 1748 had decimated the Catawba Nation, and the last epidemic killed off up to sixty percent of the tribe. The once great nation had boasted

Murder of the Greatest Catawba

King Hagler was undoubtedly an eloquent leader who won the hearts of his people and the royal governor. Like other Catawba traders, Hagler realized he could trade on his goodwill. He regularly petitioned the governor for gifts such as corn, horses, ammunition, velvet and lace clothing for his Head Men—and saddles for his daughters.

Four year before his death, Hagler's persuasive skills were evident in his request to Governor Glen in 1759: "Formerly I walked fast, but now am old and unable to walk home, therefore must beg the favour of a horse from your Excellency and as my sight is fail'd shall be obliged to you for a good gun."

Hagler was traveling from the "Waxhaws settlement on Cane Creek to a Catawba town on Twelve Mile Creek" on August 30, 1763, when he was ambushed by a band of seven Shawnee Indians—longtime enemies from Virginia. The Shawnees shot Hagler with six bullets, killing him instantly. Hagler's only companion, a slave, escaped to spread the word. Catawba drums made of deerskin stretched over clay pots broadcast the message quickly.

The location of Hagler's grave was kept secret, but Maurice Moore described it as ten feet wide, ten feet long, and ten feet deep. Hagler was buried with his silver-mounted rifle, powder flask, gold and silver coins, pipes, tobacco, and other personal possessions. According to Moore, a guard of sixteen warriors stood by his burial site for one month until a band of Virginia gamblers got the guards drunk and rifled the grave.

The Camden militia investigated the murder, and the North Carolina government sent a lieutenant with thirty men to pursue the Shawnees. They were never apprehended. The site of Hagler's murder was commemorated two centuries later with a South Carolina historical marker on Highway 5 in Lancaster County.

many thousands of warriors. In less than one hundred years, alcohol and smallpox would reduce the Catawba tribe from six thousand members to twelve hundred. Some estimate the tribe's population as low as five hundred members by the 1760s.[11]

King Hagler's loyalty didn't waver despite the many plagues whites brought to Catawba Indian Land. In less than a century, several South Carolina tribes had virtually vanished. The Yemassee Indians, who fought a bloody war with the colonists,

11) Merrell, p. 195.

had been hunted down and wiped out. Just south of the Catawba villages, the Waxhaws were killed off by disease and tribal warfare in a single generation. Most of the survivors of these vanishing cultures merged with larger tribes such as the Catawbas and the Cherokees.

The Catawbas were clearly a much weaker nation when Royal Governor of North Carolina Arthur Dobbs (1753-1763) received an order from the Board of Trade in London to convene a meeting of Indian tribes. The governors of South Carolina, North Carolina, Virginia, and Georgia met in present-day Augusta, Georgia to divide the spoils of war between five tribes—the Creeks, Choctaws, Cherokees, Chickasaws and Catawbas.

The Treaty of Augusta had been a dream of King Hagler. As early as 1757, the tribe had asked that "their lands be measured out for them."[12]

The Catawbas claimed an area within a diameter of sixty miles from their villages, but when Hagler and other Catawba leaders met with Superintendent of Indian Affairs Edmond Atkin at Pine Tree Hill in 1760, they agreed to surrender most of the land, except the area within fifteen miles. The reservation was "to be ascertained by survey, to prevent Intruders, and the Catawbas having a Fort built there at Public Expense."[13] The Catawbas would eventually abandon their six villages along the Catawba River and settle into one village on Twelve Mile Creek, where a state-funded fort was erected.

In the wake of Hagler's death, Colonel Jacob Ayres represented the Catawbas as tribal chief at Fort Augusta. The Catawbas had to wait several days while negotiations were concluded with the other tribes, and they ultimately settled for half of what they were seeking. Ayres asked for "15 miles on each side of his town free from any encroachments of white people," but he was told if the tribe did not stand behind the Treaty of Pine Tree Hill, "your claim must be undecided till our Great King's Pleasure is known on the other side of the Waters." [14]

Ayres agreed to abide by the previous treaty and he and the other tribal leaders signed the Treaty of Augusta on Nov. 5, 1763, granting the Catawbas an area of roughly "fifteen miles square," encompassing 225 square miles. Article Four of the Treaty of Augusta concerned the Catawbas:

"And We the Catawba Head Men and Warriors in Confirmation of an Agreement heretofore entered into with the White People declare that we will remain satisfied with the tract of land of Fifteen Miles square a Survey of which by our consent and at our request has been already begun and the respective Governors and Superintendent on their Parts promise and engage that the aforesaid survey shall be compleated and that the Catawbas shall not in any respect be

Disappearance of the Flat Heads

Neighboring tribes called the Waxhaw Indians "Flat Heads" because of the way they shaped their infants' heads. Believing it improved their eyesight and made them expert hunters, the Waxhaws wedged a baby's head between two bags of sand and strapped it to a board for months.

As a result of the practice, the Waxhaws' eyes "stand out a prodigious way asunder and the hair hangs over the forehead like the eaves of a house," according to surveyor John Lawson, who observed the Waxhaws in the early 1700s. Lawson described the Waxhaws as superior hosts with large cabins and a large and flourishing village on the Catawba River. But Lawson's description of the Waxhaws is the only recorded account. Within eighteen years, the Waxhaws had completely vanished—victims of a smallpox epidemic and warfare. The few who did survive most likely merged with the Catawbas.

molested by any of the King's subjects within the said Lines but shall be indulged in the usual Manner of hunting Elsewhere."[15]

A Quaker friend of King Hagler, Samuel Wyly of Camden, served as the tribe's interpreter at Fort Augusta. When Wyly surveyed the reservation the next year, he included Hagler's name on the map to honor him. He mapped out 144,000 acres, which extend across eastern York County,

12) Merrell, p. 198.
13) Brown, pp. 240-241.
14) Brown, pp. 250-251.
15) Brown, p. 251.

the "Panhandle" of Lancaster County and a half-mile-wide triangle of Chester County that resembled the point of an arrow.

The Catawbas had long referred to themselves as a "nation." With a grant to a large, fertile region of the Carolinas, the tribe took its place as a legally recognized force. The Treaty of Augusta gave the Catawbas the right to hunt anywhere in South Carolina, a dubious privilege since by 1763 the wildlife, especially deer, had been over-hunted. The Catawbas were not to be taxed and could be selective about the whites allowed to settle inside the Catawba Reservation. If their white neighbors proved to be unfriendly, the Catawbas could appeal to the British Board of Trade.

Then came the American Revolution. In 1780, nearly four years after the signing of the Declaration of Independence, the war shifted to South Carolina. After the surrender of Charleston to the British, nearly all opposition disappeared except for forces led by General Francis Marion, "The Swampfox," in the Lowcountry and General Thomas Sumter, "The Gamecock," in the Upcountry area of York and Lancaster. Sumter's men camped on the tribe's reservation at Clems Branch in present-day Lancaster County and Hagler's Hill in Fort Mill Township, and the Catawba warriors were once again called upon as allies. The tribe's women and children were moved to Virginia to stay with a friendly tribe, and

General Thomas Sumter

Catawba warriors joined Sumter's army and fought the British through the end of the war. Following Lord Cornwallis' defeat at Yorktown, Virginia, the Catawbas once again returned from war a much weaker tribe. Their abandoned villages had been pillaged and destroyed by neighboring whites and Indian enemies. Weeds had gained a foothold in the Kings Bottoms.

The Catawba soldiers had won the gratitude of state leaders, and they had made life-long friends with white soldiers with whom they served. However, times were tough, and the Catawbas wanted money to buy things such as mules, ploughs and guns. As it turned out, relationships tribal leaders cultivated during the war would be pivotal to the future of the tribe—and the leasing of Catawba Indian Land.

Revolutionary War Scouts and Spies

The Patriot militia serving in South Carolina was outnumbered, out-trained and out-gunned by British soldiers and loyalists, who were pillaging farms and businesses to stamp out opposition in the Upstate. The 500-member volunteer militia under General Thomas Sumter spent much of its time hiding from the British; however, Sumter also managed to constantly surprise and harass his enemy with guerilla tactics such as ambush and concealment, which may have been adopted from Indian warfare.

Forty-one Catawba warriors led by Captain Thomas Drennan joined Sumter's army encampment at Clems Branch on the east side of Sugar Creek in Lancaster County. While there is no record of close combat between the Indians and the British, the Catawbas deemed it very foolish to stand up against cannons or cavalry in the traditional style of European warfare. The Catawbas scouted for foodstuffs and were expert trackers. Some understood English well enough to sneak into enemy camps, climb trees and listen to the plans of the officers. Before daylight, the Catawba warriors would return to Sumter's camp with invaluable news of British plans.

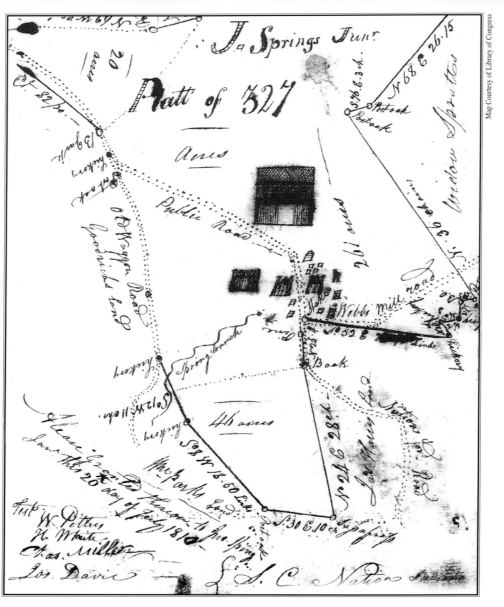

This plat for John Springs' Indian Lease shows the location of Webb's Mill, for which the town of Fort Mill was named.

Chapter Three

Land Grants, Leaseholders and Squatters

Samuel Knox arrived in the Carolinas sometime in 1763 and immediately began amassing land. Knox apparently brought considerable wealth with him for he was involved in many transactions in the Steel Creek area and across upper South Carolina as far as Spartanburg.[16] He had one sister and nine brothers, five of whom had emigrated from Ireland with their mother.

Land-hungry, like so many of the Scots-Irish immigrants, Knox settled in what would become Mecklenburg County, North Carolina, where in one year he took out patents on 3,249 acres on Steel Creek in the southwestern corner of what would become the North Carolina-South Carolina border.[17] He eventually leased 4,500 acres from the Catawbas in upper Fort Mill district and upper Lancaster County.

Another Scots-Irishman, one year younger than Knox, most likely arrived in the area sometime between 1755 and 1765. Thomas "Kanawha" Spratt (1731-1807) befriended the Catawbas on the battlefield. The Catawbas gave him the nickname "Kanawha" during an expedition to present-day West Virginia. Spratt displayed such courage that the Indians named him for the nearby Kanawha River in the same way Catawba Chief General New River earned his name.

Historians disagree on how Spratt arrived in the area. On January 15, 1751, a will by Thomas Sprot of Anson County, North Carolina left a plantation on Twelve Mile Creek "to my only son Thomas." Twelve Mile Creek in Mecklenburg County, North Carolina flowed into the Catawba River, forming the southern boundary of the Catawba Indian Land in present-day Lancaster County, South Carolina. To his daughter Martha, he left a "plantation on Sugar Creek," which led to speculation that somehow, Thomas Spratt exchanged his inheritance with his sister Martha. Other writers have said Spratt was on his way to settle in Abbeville or Fairforest (near present-day Spartanburg) when the Catawbas persuaded him to settle among them.

Spratt ultimately ended up leasing 5,175 acres of Catawba land in present-day Fort Mill Township, where he built a home and raised a family. While Spratt did not technically have a Catawba lease, he had a "contract" that indicates he received a large acreage in exchange for recruiting other settlers, who would presumably pro-

16) North Carolina patents alone accounted for Knox's buying and selling 8,048 acres between the dates of April 19, 1763 and October 3, 1775.
17) Knox's initial acquisitions were made in three purchases filed on April 19, 1763, and four purchases filed on December 21, 1763. Margaret Hoffmann, Colony of North Carolina, 1735-1764, Abstracts of Land Patents, Vol. 1 (Roanoke News Company, Weldon, N.C., 1982)

Samuel Knox's Stately Brick House

While Samuel Knox did not serve in the military, he was recognized as an "American Patriot" by the Daughters of the American Revolution. One of Samuel Knox's relations, John Rosser, described him as "a great man of the family in the country." Knox built his family a brick house, which Rosser said was "probably the first brick house for that purpose ever built in that country."

After his death in 1800, Knox's estate was distributed to his widow, Mary Taggart Knox, three daughters, and the grandchildren living in 1794 when he made his will. The daughters each received one-third of Knox's 4,500 acres of leased Indian land. Knox's "favorite" daughter, Sarah, married Alexander Candlish and lived on the land for three or four years before moving to St. Mary's, Georgia. Her sisters, Jane and Mary, married two brothers and settled in Catawba Indian Land. Jane married Captain George Pettus and Mary became the wife of William Pettus.

Knox is buried beside his mother and several of his young children in the Steele Creek Presbyterian Church cemetery in Mecklenburg County, North Carolina. Knox's widow, who died many years later in 1828, is believed to be buried in the Pettus family cemetery north of Fort Mill, South Carolina.

vide money, supplies and services such as protection against invasion from enemy tribes.[18] All evidence points to his being "invited" by the Catawbas (as his grandson wrote) or, at least, when Spratt arrived, he was heartily accepted by the Catawbas.

Up to two-thirds of the Catawba Indian Land settlers prior to the end of the Revolutionary War came from the North— at that time, North Carolina, Virginia and Pennsylvania.[19] Like Knox and Spratt, most were Scots-Irish. All of the churches founded in Catawba Indian Land prior to the Revolution were Presbyterian, founded by Scots-Irish congregations.

Between the 1740s and the 1770s, many of these new South Carolina settlers arrived thinking they were living in North Carolina. Many had received North Carolina patents, or land grants. The Crown had decreed that the boundary line between North and South Carolina be drawn as early as 1734, but surveying difficulties had halted the effort and mistakenly drawn the boundary line east of the Catawba River eleven miles south of the designated 35th parallel. The survey was abandoned until 1772. During that time, North Carolina's Land Office granted a considerable amount of acreage presently in South Carolina from 1748 until the 1772 survey.

Some of the North Carolina patents clearly situate the property within the Catawba Indian Land, such as the patent for

Christian Erwin on August 30, 1753: "400 acres in Anson County on Cataba river and the Waggon Ford at the Cataba Nation, joining both sides of the river." However, there is no way to be certain that Erwin actually settled on the land.[20]

Nor is there proof that Richard Graham settled on patented land that was clearly within the Catawba Indian's grant: "Richard Graham, 17 May 1754, 300 acres in Anson County on the South Side of the Cataba River, joining the sd. River and (a point) above the Mouth of Dutchmans Creek Opposite to the Nation." A patent for Mary Kuykindall on March 26, 1755, granted 280 acres "in Anson County on the N. side of the Dutchmans creek on or near Abraham Kuykindalls line, joining James Kuykindall."[21]

Strangely, one North Carolina patent for land in present-day Lancaster County was recorded in a York County Deed Book for 200 acres on "both sides 12 Mile Creek opposite Catawba Indian town."[22] The York County deed was recorded in 1786, although the original North Carolina patent was dated November 18, 1752, and issued to William Edey. Edey sold the land to Robert Barkley who sold to William Hagins in July 1756. Hagins then sold to John Drennan on October 10, 1765. The York County Registrar recorded the deed under the names of "William Haggins and wf. Mary of Waxhaws and Mecklenburg

18) John M. Spratt, Jr., a descendant, has a typewritten copy of a lease dated August 25, 1795, between the Head Men of the Catawba Nation and John Robison and Robert Harris, which contains the word "contract" to describe an agreement made by King Hagler, Colonel Ears, and other chiefs of the Catawba Nation with Thomas Spratt "about the year 1765." Another paper apparently refers to the contract ending and on February 9, 1787, designated as the date "from which time separate rent did commence." 19) Robert L. Meriwether, The Expansion of South Carolina, 1729-1765. 20) Ibid. #364, p. 26. 21) Ibid, #4477, p. 320 22) York County Deed Book A #14, pp. 29-32.

Thomas "Kanawha" Spratt: Promoter and Protector

Under his contractual relationship with the tribe, Thomas Spratt was responsible for recruiting white settlers to lease part of Catawba Indian Land. As one of the first Indian agents, Spratt witnessed many Catawba leases and protected tribal members against unscrupulous traders. According to legend, he adopted several Indian children including Peter Harris, a Catawba whose parents died in a smallpox epidemic. Harris is buried in the Spratt family graveyard on Brickyard Road in Fort Mill, not far from Spratt's grave.

Spratt and his wife Elizabeth Bigger raised seven daughters and one son in Catawba Indian Land: Mary; Martha, who married Isaac Garrison; Elizabeth, who married Hugh White; Jane who married Thomas McNeal; Anne; James, who married Margaret McRee; Susannah, who married Joseph McCorkle; and Rachel, who married Arthur Erwin.

While some Spratt descendants migrated westward seeking better cotton lands in the pre-Civil war period, a large number remained in York County.

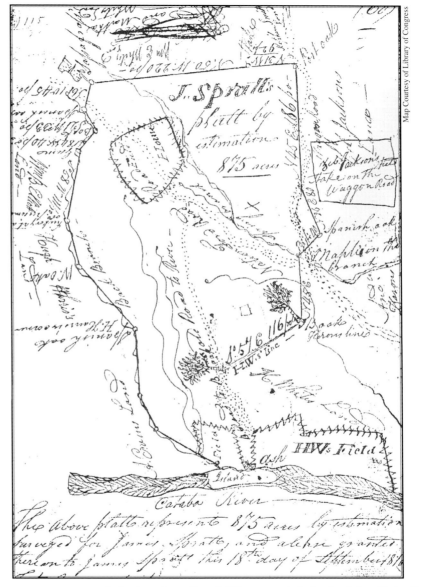

A plat shows James Spratt's 875-acre tract in Indian Land along Nation Ford Road, just north of an island in the Catawba River.

County, N.C., and John Drennan, late of Pennsylvania." On December 24, 1765, the deed was amended with a nota bene (a legal device to point out particularly important facts) that stated: "The Indians claim is excepted only the nota bene done before signing." The note in essence meant that Hagins had no right to assign title to Drennan on his own.

Hagins, who arrived in the area in 1745, acquired large amounts of acreage in Mecklenburg County and the Waxhaws of Lancaster County. Like many of the first settlers, he received North Carolina patents prior to the establishment of the Indian boundary in 1763.

North Carolina's land patents distressed the Catawbas who hoped to put a stop to them with the Treaty of Augusta. In exchange for signing the treaty, Colonel Ayres said once the survey was made, "the People settled within should be removed and no new warrants granted them or any others to settle within those Limits."[23]

After Samuel Wyly's survey of the reservation in 1764, the province of North Carolina had no authority to issue patents in Catawba Indian Land, yet it would be eight years before the North Carolina-South Carolina boundary line was surveyed, a situation that was bound to cause future problems.

For every settler who bothered to secure a North Carolina patent, there were probably three or four who did not. These trespassers, or squatters, tended to avoid the Catawba villages and settle some distance away, especially on the fringes of Wyly's western survey lines. Isaac Smith, for example, waited until 1787 to record the 1757 survey of his 615 3/4 acres. Most likely, other "fringe settlers" moved into area west of the Catawba River—as far from the Indian towns as possible. Eventually, they recorded their holdings with the Indian Commissioners and began rent payments to the Catawbas.[27]

During the colonial era, long before the government-sanctioned leaseholder system began in 1785, court records indicate numerous leases had been arranged with settlers, many of whom were already subleasing their land. In his York County will on March 9, 1787, Francis Smartt left a Catawba lease to his son George Smartt, with the statement that he had already paid fourteen years of rent to the Indians. Robert Patton's will on March 4, 1779, referenced a Catawba Indian lease for land adjacent to John Walker and John Barnett. On October 23, 1779, Samuel McClelan Sr. deeded leased land to his son, Samuel Jr., except for "the part now leased to John Sturgis."[28]

The first colonial leases were probably little more than a handshake. The Catawbas had existed for centuries as communal vil-

23) Letter from John M. Spratt, Jr. to the author, January 14, 2002. 24) Known recipients of North Carolina patents inside the Catawba reservation included eleven on Dutchmans Creek which empties into the west bank of the Catawba River and four patents on the Lancaster side of the Catawba. (See appendix p. 67 for names.) 25) Margaret M. Hofmann, Colony of North Carolina, 1753-1764: Abstracts of Land Patent, Volume One, Weldon, N. C.: The Roanoke News Company, 1982.
26) Letter from John M. Spratt, Jr. to the author, January 14, 2002. 27) The loss of the record books kept by Charles Miller and Josina Garrison results in far less certainty about the leasing history of the west side of the Catawba river compared to the records preserved by the heirs of Hugh White, who kept the records on the east side of the Catawba.
28) The deed was not recorded until July 10, 1790, more than ten years later. York County Deed Book B #111, pp. 236-37.

North Carolina's Illegal Land Grants

At least fifteen North Carolina land patents were granted to white men illegally—without the consent of the Catawba leaders—between 1763 (Treaty of Augusta) and 1772 (the survey of the North Carolina-South Carolina boundary line).[24] Prior to 1763, patents that were very likely within Catawba Indian Land were held by Thomas Lovick, David Huston, William Barnett, James Armour, Christian Erwin, Robert Clenachan, Matthew Patton, Hugh Cunningham, Casper Culp, Thomas Patton, Richard Graham, James Sharp, Mary Kuykendall, John Patton and James Weakley.[25]

There are no records that prove any of the North Carolina patent holders actually lived on their land. However, the surnames of Barnett, Erwin, Clenachan [McClenahan], Patton, Culp, Kuykendal and Graham resurface on Catawba Indian leases twenty to thirty years later, indicating these leaseholders were the sons or grandsons of the original North Carolina patent holders. Under North Carolina law, the recipient of the patent was required to cultivate at least three acres out of each one hundred acres granted. This law may explain why Thomas Spratt allowed 390 acres of his inherited Twelve Mile Creek tract to revert to North Carolina in favor of the much more generous offer from the Catawba Indians.[26]

William Ervin's Quest for Milk and Butter

An early Fort Mill settler, William Ervin was one of the white colonists recruited by Thomas Spratt to move to Catawba Indian Land. And it appears to be a decision Ervin would later regret.

Ervin's family traveled to Fort Mill from Virginia, and through Spratt's influence with the Catawbas, he was able to obtain a lease of three miles square extending from the Steel Creek bridge on toward Charlotte. Ervin probably raised some of the area's first dairy cattle, but the venture met with disastrous consequences. Distemper wiped out his entire stock, but Ervin was undaunted:

"He bought a fresh supply, for he could not, he declared, live without milk and butter. The distemper again visited his range. The third time he bought more, the distemper killed every cow. In thorough disgust, he sold three miles square of Indian land for an Indian pony, a silver watch, a whiskey still and an old wagon, shook the dust off his feet, and removed to the head waters of Turkey Creek near the spot where Yorkville now stands and where his cattle found immunity from disease."[29]

29) Maurice Moore, Reminiscences of York, p. 14.

lage dwellers with common lands for hunting and crops. None of the land was subdivided. The concept of land ownership was completely new to the Catawbas, but the Treaty of Augusta dramatically altered the way individual tribal members viewed the land. Land leasing gave them another way to make the white settlers' money so they could buy more of the white settlers' goods.

Many of the early suitors for the tribe's land, such as William Henry Drayton, viewed the Catawbas as uneducated, assuming the Indians could be easily swindled.

Drayton, a member of the South Carolina Council and a powerful Lowcountry family, appeared on the reservation on January 8, 1773, with an offer to lease the entire reservation. Drayton told the Head Men of the tribe that if they would give him a 21-year lease, he would "be a father to them" and protect them from abuse. Drayton planned to rent out the land to white settlers and provide every warrior with necessary supplies every year. At first, the Catawbas were inclined to accept the proposal, not understanding that Drayton intended to take over the entire reservation.

Drayton had planned carefully. He had persuaded the royal governor and the council to back his scheme.[30] Fortunately for the Catawbas, John Stuart, the Crown's appointed superintendent, objected to Drayton's plans and persuaded the council to reverse its decision.

Interest in the Catawba Indian Land increased after the end of the Revolutionary War. The Catawbas were said to welcome Whig veterans, and if they discovered the newcomers had supported the English, they refused to rent their land to them and drove them away. Catawba Indian Land became home to many veterans who had served General Sumter when he camped at Clems Branch and Hagler's Hill. David Hutchison, one of the early settlers, was an old man when he reminisced in 1843:

"About this time (early 1780s) a large number of young men, chiefly from Mecklenburg County who had served six or eight years in the Army, returned home poor and penniless. A number of them had served their last tour in Sumter's State troops—privates receiving a Negro, and officers in proportion to their rank; and this was their all. In the course of two years, the most of these men married. In camp they became acquainted with a number of Indians and were favorites with them. These men when married, being without means sufficient to purchase improved land, were encouraged by the Indians and whites already settled to come and live on their land; which most of them did, purchasing from the first settlers; and thus

commenced in the woods, poor in property, but rich in independence of mind."[31]

While Catawbas began reaping rewards from land leases, they were becoming increasingly alarmed about the number of settlers flocking to the area and nibbling off parts of their land. Three years before a state-sanctioned leasing system began, two Catawbas traveled to the Continental Congress seeking federal protection to prevent whites from forcefully taking portions of their land. The petition sought protection against intrusion or alienation "even with their own consent." This early appeal for assistance went unanswered. The Continental Congress referred the matter to the South Carolina Legislature to "take such measures for the satisfaction and security of the said tribe as the said legislature shall, in their wisdom, think fit." Eight years later, Congress would approve the Indian Trade and Intercourse Act of 1790, which gave Congress the authority over treaties with Indian tribes. The law, referred to as the Non-Intercourse Act, was amended three years later to provide:

"… no purchase or grant of lands … from any Indians or nation or tribe of Indians, within the boundary of the United States, shall be of any validity in law or equity, unless the same be made by a treaty or convention entered into pursuant to the constitution … [and] in the presence, and with the approbation of the commissioners of the United States."

30) Wyly to Kershaw, Jan 28[?], 1773, and encl., Kershaw Papers.
31) David Hutchison letter written at the request of South Carolina Governor James Hammond, dated July 11, 1843.

Governor William Moultrie

following the war. Many parts of Upstate South Carolina had no laws. There were no courts and no officers to keep the peace. The Catawbas and a scattered community of white leaseholders were living on the frontier.

Two years after the end of the Revolutionary War, the state's most powerful politician began pushing for the settlement of Catawba Indian Land. William Moultrie, a general and a hero of the American Revolution, was elected first governor of the state of South Carolina. In his "State of the State" address to the South Carolina General Assembly on February 17, 1785, Governor Moultrie made a series of recommendations on the fledgling state's needs in agriculture, trade, "public credit," and how to handle the Catawba Indian matter. About one-third of Governor Moultrie's short address was devoted to his vision of helping the tribe by allowing six or seven hundred white families to lease Catawba land:

"Some Years ago the Governor and Council of this Country allotted to the Catawba Nation of Indians a large tract of rich, fertile lands of fourteen miles and a half Square on our Northern Boundary, a very inconsiderable part of which, is made any use of either by their Occupancy or Cultivation. I therefore humbly Suggest for your Consideration, the leasing out those lands (with their Concurrence) in Small Tracts; the Yearly Rents to be applied Solely to their Maintenance

and Support, and for the establishing of Schools among them for the Education of their Children; by this they will become an enlightened Civilized People and usefull Inhabitants of the State, and the land afford Comfortable, Profitable settlements for Six or Seven hundred families,[32] and leave an Ample Sufficiency for the Present Possessors; this will greatly increase our Population and Produce, but if they are Suffered to live in their present Ignorant uncivilized manner; they will be a burthen to the State, and the land remain uncultivated, and an useless Forest for many years."[33]

Later that year, the state-sanctioned Catawba Indian Land leaseholder system began. The first recorded lease was awarded to Samuel Knox on November 15, 1785—ten months after Governor Moultrie unveiled his plan. It was the same year the South Carolina Legislature created counties such as York, Lancaster and Chester and lawmakers adjusted tax rates to ensure backcountrymen were taxed less per acre than prosperous rice plantation owners. The market for the wholesale leasing of the Catawbas' land was open, and over the next fifty-five years, it would become big business.

The Non-Intercourse Act was written to ensure states and local jurisdictions were dealing fairly with the Indians, and it would prove pivotal to the Catawbas' land claim over the next two centuries. Despite its expressed authority over Indian affairs, Congress obviously looked upon the plight of the Catawbas as a South Carolina problem. At the time, South Carolina's legislature was embroiled in the arduous task of setting up a new government in the chaos

---

32) The leasing system came to an end in 1840 with the Treaty of Nation Ford. At that time each leaseholder was required to submit a survey to the Secretary of State who would then issue a state grant to the former leaseholder. The total number of surveys that resulted was 508.

33) Journals of the House of Representatives 1785-1786, Lark Emerson Adams, ed., Published by the South Carolina Department of Archives and History and the University of South Carolina Press, 1979.

eob Scot General Jacob Ayres Colonel
and John G. Brown Capt & Henry
l head men and acting chiefs of the Cataweba
Polk have Set our hands & seals this date

Jacob his
mark Scot Genl [Seal]

Jacob his
mark Ayres Colonel [Seal]

Thomas his
mark Brown Magor [Seal]

John G. his
mark Brown Cap [Seal]

Henry his
mark White Lewis [Seal]

The bottom of the Polk/Bedon lease shows the marks of the Catawba Head Men. One of the commissioners typically wrote out the names and witnessed each mark, which was certified by the state seal.

Chapter Four

The Leaseholder System

*I*n many ways, the signing of a Catawba Indian Land lease was a community event. To prepare for the signing of a new lease, a state-appointed Indian commissioner posted public notices in the neighborhood, inviting all interested parties. At the appointed hour, as many as five Indian commissioners, four tribal Head Men, the parties involved in the transaction and their neighbors would meet in the immediate area, probably at someone's home.[34]

To make the lease legally binding, the state required the signatures of the Catawba Head Men and at least three of the five state-appointed commissioners. The Catawba Head Men usually signed with their marks, which were witnessed by two whites, including one of the commissioners.

While the ink was drying, it's likely the men shared a convivial jug of whiskey before parting, as was the custom.

These informal gatherings vastly differed from the traditional practice of recording a deed at the county courthouse. The transfer of a deed typically involved only the buyer, the seller, a surveyor and court officials. It's unlikely lawyers were ever present at the signing of a Catawba lease. The process was managed by the commissioners, most of whom were merely well-respected farmers and businessmen with varying degrees of education. Instead of the county courthouse in Yorkville, the survey plats were recorded in the Indian Book, which was kept at the home of one of the commissioners. Presumably, the five commissioners elected one of their own to "keep the book."

Although the first book was lost, testimony in a court case in 1830 identified the first keeper and the first leaseholder: "The first entry in the Indian book is in the handwriting of Charles Miller who was an agent all his life, and this entry is to Mr. Knox."[35] In 1808 Indian Commissioner Hugh White began keeping the Surveyor's Plat Book and Indian Commissioner's Rent Book, which held copies of the plats and records of rents paid to the Catawbas on the east side of river.[36] Each time the lease changed hands, an endorsement was made on the back. It is doubtful that the Catawbas received copies of the leases, which were retained by the leaseholders.

Record keeping was haphazard at best. The keeper of the book had no authority to mandate the recording of every plat. The

---

34) Bill 63, York District Equity Court, filed January 9, 1822.
35) York County Chancery Court, Bill No. 60, "Alexander Sutton vs. John Jackson," April 20, 1830.
36) A microfilmed copy of the Surveyor's Plat Book and Indian Commissioner's Rent Book is available at the South Carolina Department of Archives and History.

state left that responsibility to the lessee, who was expected to have the land surveyed and take the plat to the commissioner for copying into the book. Travel was difficult in the early days of the leaseholder period, and many of the squatters did not bother to make their occupation official.

The system was hardly efficient, and the process of bringing all of the parties together for the lease signing was inconvenient. Therefore, it is no surprise that soon after the appointment of the first five superintendents, leaseholders in York County were openly complaining about the leasing system. In 1787 forty inhabitants of York County's Indian Land petitioned the state legislature for the appointment of new superintendents:

"… it is the Opinion of your Petitioners that a Number of said men so Chosen live too Remote from us, and Others we humbly Consider not so well Qualified for the Trust Reposed in them."[37]

The Catawbas, who also complained about the leaseholder system, first asked the state legislature for assistance in 1792. Some leaseholders were selling or subleasing parts of their property, and the new tenants were refusing to pay the Catawbas. Frustrated by the number of squatters on their land, the Catawbas petitioned the legislature to give the Indian Commissioners greater authority to identify the squatters and force them to pay rent:

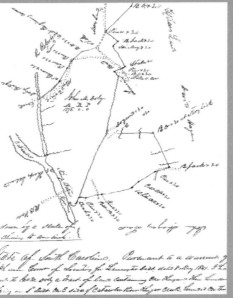

Sally New River's Lease: Fit for a Queen

Sally New River was a beloved Catawba queen, the wife of the great war hero and chief, General New River, who died sometime around 1804. She was a relatively well-to-do Catawba Indian. According to the Surveyor's Plat Book and Indian Commissioner's Rent Book, she collected rent from eight different leaseholders—William B. Elliott, Samuel Elliott, James Spratt, Andrew Herron, Hugh White, Martha White, and William E. White.

Sally New River owned 502 acres in the fertile Kings Bottoms granted by the Head Men of the tribe for her support of "good causes." In what was likely an attempt to preserve the tribe's prime farmland for future generations, the lease was recorded in the Lancaster County courthouse on April 14, 1808. Her lease to part of the Kings Bottoms is the only known lease recorded by a Catawba Indian in a courthouse:

"WITNESSTH that the said head men of the said Nation for and inconsideration of Divers good causes unto them done by her the said Sally New River have granted aliened and confirmed and by their presents do grant alien and confirm unto her the sd Sally New River her with other women of the Sd Nation themselves their heirs successors or assigns forever all that messuage tract or parcel of Land Situated and lying on a tract or parcel of Land Fifteen Miles Square to them granted by the government & now by the States, lying and adjoining the Cattawba River …"

The lease granted perpetual rights to Sally New River, "other women of said nation, and their heirs."[38] About six years after her death, however, Betsy and Sally Ayres, represented by Lewis Cantey, leased the Kings Bottoms to John M. Doby on October 29, 1824. The second lease, which was contrary to Sally New River's intentions, was recorded in the commissioners' book, not the courthouse.

37) See Appendix p. 67.
38) Lancaster County Court Records, signed on April 6, 1796, by three Catawba Head Men, General New River, Colonel John Ears (Ayres), and Major John Brown, and four commissioners, Charles Miller, Andrew Foster, Thomas Spratt, and Hugh White.

"... what we do Desire of those who have Sold part of Lands we have leased to them is to pay their Contracts and those who have purchased to pay Rents to us—as it might be Judged Equitable as it may Destroy our land to have so many Improvements thereon and not Receive Sufficient Benefits according to Rates we have always consented to Rent it: also there is a Disagreeable circumstance that we are Difficulted to prove our Right to that which is our own. We therefore beseech your Honourable House to take our Situation into Consideration and give further Power & Authority to our Agents that have been appointed to adjust us in our affairs Viz: Charles Miller, Thomas Spratt, Andrew Foster, Hugh Whitesides & Nathaniel Irvin. That you would please to give them Commissions on our behalf that they may be enabled to Regulate and order all our affairs in whatever can be done for us ..."

Over the next decade, the Catawbas lost confidence in the commissioners. On November 25, 1805, the acting chiefs of the tribe—Gen. Jacob Scott, Col. Jacob Ears, Major George Canty, Capt. Thomas Cook, Capt. William Scott, Capt. Peter George and Capt. Billy Brown—asked the legislature to allow the tribe to appoint new commissioners:

"[The commissioners] become old and much impaired in their health and have declined our business for some time past ... we beseech your honors to issue a new Commission upon that old decree and leave the Blanks for us to fix Such names to it, as we shall choose ..."[39]

George Washington

A major flaw in the leasing system was the absence of legal authority. Some of the leases were recorded in both the commissioners' book and at the county courthouse. For example, the sheriff sometimes recorded the sale of a Catawba lease at the courthouse as a result of a lawsuit that led to the auctioning off of leaseholder property. However, the court had no legal authority to enforce the terms of the leases or liens associated with the property.

Outside the court's jurisdiction, white inhabitants of the Catawba Indian Land surely felt they were living in a no-man's

No Sympathy From George Washington

Catawba Indian warriors had fought and died in Gen. George Washington's army. After the war, surviving Catawba leaders appealed to him for protection from encroaching settlers. When President Washington toured Southern states and passed through Catawba Indian Land on May 27, 1791, he wrote in his diary about his meeting with tribal leaders at Major Robert Crawford's home:

"I was met by some chiefs of the Cutawba Nation who seemed to be under apprehension that some attempts were making or would be to deprive them of part of the 40,000 [sic] Acres wch. was secured to them by Treaty and wch. is bounded by this Road."[40]

Washington apparently made no commitments to the Catawbas, nor did he ever indicate any sympathy. Five years later, the tribe sent a delegation to camp on the grounds of his home at Mount Vernon, Virginia. In the last year of his presidency on July 18, 1796, Washington indicated to Secretary of War James McHenry that the Catawbas had overstayed their welcome:

"I have already been incommoded, at this place, by a visit of several days, from a party of a dozen Cuttawbas; & should wish while I am in this retreat, to avoid a repetition of such guests."[41]

---

39) There is no direct evidence that the legislature responded to the petition, nor is there evidence that points directly to the individuals to whom the Indians objected.
40) NAME OF PUBLICATION Donald Jackson, ed. and Dorothy Twohig, ed. p. 149. President Washington erred in thinking the tribe held 40,000 acres. The total was 144,000 acres.
41) Ibid, p. 150.

Indian Land residents complained they had "escaped the notice of" legislators in the State Capitol.

Revolutionary War protests against "taxation without representation" when they told legislators they had "done our duty as citizens, we serve on juries, we are obedient to the military Law, we pay our county tax for the support of the poor, and for the public buildings."[42] There is no known response to the request. Certainly, there was no election.

Adding insult to injury, the legislature in 1802 required that slaves working on land leased from the Catawbas were to be taxed at the usual rates—"fifty cents per head … levied on all slaves" and two dollars per head on "all free negroes, mulattoes, and mestizos between the ages of sixteen and fifty years."[43]

Lack of representation was also a source of resentment for residents of Lancaster County's Indian Land. In a complaint still echoed today by local politicians, a group of Lancaster County leaseholders criticized the legislature for ignoring the region:

"A moiety of the State to the Eastward of the Catawba River and between the Mouth of the Twelve Mile Creek and the North Carolina line (in which bounds the petitioners reside) seemed to have escaped the notice of the Legislature, by which means the petitioners are left without Officers either Civil or Military or any legal means for a redress of Grievances ..."[44]

In practice, the people of the Lancaster section of the Catawba Indian Land still had no government. The legislature's solution

land. No townships were established in Catawba Indian land, and the only official government was a militia unit. A captain of the militia, who recruited his company from the local population, presided over "beats" within the reservation. The captain's authority over the civilians was not defined. Members of the militia could elect their own officers and were expected to serve on county juries. However, they did not have the right to vote for local, state or national

officeholders because they were not "freeholders," who according to state constitution had to own a state grant of at least five hundred acres. Ironically, the Catawba Indians, who controlled 144,000 acres, could not vote either.

In 1795, 148 leaseholders in York County petitioned for the right to elect a representative to the state legislature. Representing an estimated 350 families, the petitioners were probably reminded of

---

42) York County leaseholders petition to the S.C. House of Representatives, 1795-03-01. The leaseholders also paid $2.00 in taxes per slave. See appendix p. 67 for names of the 148 leaseholders who signed the petition.
43) S.C. Statutes at Large, Vol. 5.
44) Statutes of South Carolina, No. 2034 (Vol. V., p. 697-698). The white settlers in the area described, still called Indian Land, were not recognized as having rights of voters or office holders until 1819.

for this problem was only a partial one. A committee was appointed to look into the matter of which county, York or Lancaster, should become responsible for the panhandle area. For the first time, the state established a militia, "commanded by Captains Massey and Moore," to keep the peace inside Lancaster County Indian Land.[45]

In 1808 York County leaseholders took matters into their own hands. They elected William Pettus, one of Samuel Knox's heirs, as their representative to the state legislature. Pettus carried a plan to Columbia that would correct the faults of the old leasing system, but the House of Representatives refused to seat him. He could not serve in the House because the state constitution required members to be freeholders. Pettus held leases for at least 1,500 acres but he did not hold title to any land.[46] The voters who elected him also were ineligible.

In 1808 the legislature placed tighter regulations on the leaseholder system—most likely in response to Pettus' proposal. The act allowed the Catawbas to grant leases either for the life of the lessee or for a term up to ninety-nine years, but limited the amount of rent they could collect in advance.[47] It required the appointment of five commissioners with three of them required to witness each lease and at least four Catawba "Head Men" to sign the agreement.[48] Commissioners were to be appointed for seven-year terms.

The new leasing restrictions were implemented by 1810, the year Pettus was ultimately seated in the legislature, where he would serve three terms. Years later, John Springs wrote that an early office holder was forced to buy five hundred acres of poor land outside of Indian Land in order to be seated. Springs may have meant Pettus but most likely he was referring to Thomas Robertson, who lived near the southern boundary of Catawba Indian Land. Robertson served three terms in the legislature between 1809 and 1817.[49]

Residents of northern Lancaster County also gained rights as citizens. In 1813 the Lancaster District recognized leaseholders north of Twelve Mile Creek and allowed them to vote, serve on juries and become members of the militia.

While the white settlers were finally getting more rights, the legislature was placing greater restrictions on the Catawbas. The new leasing restrictions prohibited settlers from paying the Catawbas more than three years of rent payments in advance. It was intended to protect the Catawbas from wasting their proceeds. Many settlers feared tribal members would spend the money on whiskey. David Hutchison, an influential leader in Indian Land, would later blame the Catawbas' dependency on alcohol on the abundance of stills built by white farmers who produced more grain than they could market.

The restriction against collecting more than three years of rent in advance drew protests from the tribal Head Men in the form of a petition to the legislature labeled "Grievances" on November 30, 1810:

"… there are many separate tracts of our land at from two to ten Dollars annually and in consequence of the said clause of three years many of our leasees have it not in their power to pay to our said Nations anything but some small trifles that is easily squandered away or of but little use to us. We therefore pray your Honorable body to repeal that part of the Act and allow our leasees the privilege of to our said Nation Seven or Eight years in advance and your petitions or in duty bound will ever pray."[50]

Their request to extend the down payments to seven or eight years was not granted. There were few other restrictions on the system. Catawba tribal members could lease their land to anyone they wished at varying rates under the general supervision of the commissioners and tribal Head Men.

Rent payments were made to individual Indians, including women and children, upon whom lay the burden of collection. The commissioners were only required to record the rents paid and settle disputes brought to them. However, most of the disputes were between adjoining white leaseholders, generally over boundary lines—not

45) The North Carolina-South Carolina boundary line was surveyed by a joint team from each state in 1813.
46) Samuel Knox, the father-in-law of William Pettus, had died in 1800 and Pettus had inherited one-third of Knox's lease holdings. 47) S.C. Statutes at Large, V, Act 1926, pp. 576-577. 48) Only one Catawba, John Nettles, actually signed his name. The others used symbols that represented their clans. 49) Biographical Directory of the South Carolina House of Representatives, Vol IV. Pettus biography, pp. 440-41; Robertson biography, pp. 483-84. 50) Signed by thirteen Catawba officers each affixing his individual mark: Jacob Scott, Brig. Genl; Jacob Ears, Collo; John Nettles, Major; Thos. Cook, Capt.; Henry White, Capt.; Mose Ears, Capt.; Billey Redhead, John Dudgeon, Billey Ears, Jenet Brown, Isaac White; James Clinton and James Brown. Three of the five state-appointed superintendents witnessed the document: Hugh White, Charles Miller and George Massey.

between the whites and the Catawbas.

Three decades after the first lease was officially recorded, the legislature finally addressed the problem of squatters, or trespassers, on the Catawbas' land in 1815.[51] Under the Trespass Act, the Indian commissioners were authorized to "prosecute an action or actions of trespass to try titles to the lands claimed by and vested in the said Indians, that is now or may hereafter be held in possession by any person or persons, without a lease from the head men or chiefs of the said nation of Indians. "

The act required the commissioners to keep a record of the rents collected and compelled trespassers to pay for any damages to the Indians' personal property.

While the Catawbas had the right to resolve lease disputes in court, they apparently preferred to take such matters to the commissioners or appeal directly to the legislature, as they had done in the past. In 1800 a petition to the legislature over a boundary dispute between two leases demonstrated this preference:

"(We) … Pray that you would take some Measures in order to compromise the Matter in dispute as we are not fond of Quarrells nor suits of that Nature whatsoever."[52]

The state still viewed the Catawbas as a sovereign nation, but by 1820 the tribe was only a fraction of its former size. Some estimates of the population were as low

as one hundred members.[53] The Catawbas realized they no longer could stymie the ever-increasing number of land-hungry white men.

Two years after the Trespass Act, the Catawbas sent notice to the legislature to quell rumors that thirty young men of the tribe had left the state to affiliate themselves with "wandering tribes." Tribal leaders said the report was completely unfounded "for the purpose of making our Legislative Body believe that we rest unsatisfy'd under their government." The Catawbas reassured legislators that:

"… our Young Warriors are all at home and following their Common Employment … [and] we and them are determined to live on our native lands and support the government of our native country and of the State of South Carolina as long as we have life and Means to go upon in support of the same …"[54]

The petition was signed by nine Catawbas including Revolutionary War heroes Brigadier General Jacob Scott, Colonel Jacob Ayers and Captain Thomas Cook; an interpreter, Peter Harris, the adopted son of Thomas "Kanawha" Spratt; and John Nettles, who had attended William and Mary College in Virginia. Obviously, the Catawbas did not want to antagonize the authorities in any way.

Even with more state oversight, however, problems with the leasing system per-

Fisticuffs in the Mulberry Fields Between Spratt and Knox

As Catawba Indian Land became more populated, boundary disputes were bound to happen. One of the earliest instances of such a dispute was cited in Thomas Dryden Spratt's Recollections, an anecdotal account of the lives of his grandfather, Thomas "Kanawha" Spratt, and father, James Spratt. The elder Spratt had a violent dispute with Samuel Knox over a river tract below Neely's Ferry called the mulberry fields:

"This controversy terminated in a fight between the two. I have heard that they rolled over and over one another down a hill, from a spring on the premises, some fifty or more yards. Some of Knox's descendants hold that he got the better of the fight, but memory serves one to the effect that it was a drawn battle."

Although no date for the altercation was provided, even if the fight occurred in 1785, the year Knox obtained his lease, neither leaseholder was very young. The two feuding men would have been in their mid-50s.

51) Statutes at Large Vol. VI, No. 2093. AN ACT to authorize and empower the Superintendents of the Catawba Indians to institute Actions for Trespasses on their Land; and for other purposes therein mentioned, pp. 18-19.
52) Dispute between George Pettus and Joseph Davis. Transcribed by Margaret Elmore Turner on October 11, 1994, from the original document signed by forty-nine Catawbas, dated July 10, 1800.
53) Charles Hudson, The Catawba Nation, p, 51.
54) "Resolves of Meeting by the Headmen of the Catawba Nation, York and Lancaster Districts," 23rd Nov. 1817."

sisted. In 1821 the tribe sent yet another petition to the legislature. This time, leaseholders were pressuring the Catawbas to renew their leases with more favorable terms:

"We … have rented to the white people nearly all their Lands for the term of ninety nine years but the white people hath called upon the indians diferent times to renew their Leaces which the indians did, not knowing that it was for the purpose of making their Leaces Live any Longer then our first agreement."

Once again tribal leaders repeated their grievances against trespassers and squatters:

"… the indians believe their is Some of their Land that they nor their fathers have never Leaced to the white people which they (the whites) Claim and are in possesion of the indians pray that all parts of their Lands that they have not Leaced to the white people within twenty years and regular rents been paid to us may be put in our possession that we may Either Cultivate it ourselves or Leace it to whom we think fit. . . . "[55]

In this instance, none of the state-appointed commissioners signed the petition, in contrast to their usual support for the Indians' complaints. In their petitions to the legislature the Indians never specifically identified the white men who were cheating them. No court records have been found that indicate who took advantage of them or whether they were ever compelled to pay back rent.

To protect the Catawbas' rights, the leases became more specific over time and clearly spelled out penalties for non-payment. For example, William Potts' lease in 1826 included the statement that if rent was in arrears more than six months "it is clearly understood and expressly agreed by both the Contracting Parties at the time of assigning of these presents that the chiefs and headmen of the Catawba Indians can reenter and possess and enjoy the said premises as fully and as completely as if this Lease had never existed."

The leasing system clearly had checks and balances to ensure the Catawbas had legally enforceable agreements. It's doubtful, however, that the Catawbas ever received fair market value for their land.

---

55) "The Petition of the Chiefs and Head men of the Tribe of Catawba Indians praying that certain Leases made of their Territory may be investigated & their grievances redressed" was addressed to the Judiciary committee of the South Carolina House of Representatives.

Chapter Five

The Business of Catawba Indian Leases

Catawba Indian land leases were undoubtedly the only way for many Upstate families to establish a farm with very little money down. The Catawbas typically leased their land for $1.50 to $10 a year for tracts ranging from 100 acres to 1,800 acres. Most leases ran for ninety-nine years, but in many cases, the leaseholders got a substantial discount for the first decade or more.

For example, William Moore rented 951 acres in 1819 on northwest side of the Saluda Road for 50 cents a year "or the value in goods or chattels" through 1830—due on the first day of January. For the remainder of the ninety-nine year lease, the rent increased to $4 a year. One 365-acre tract was leased in 1804 to Robert Lesley, as guardian of Thomas Neel, for a horse valued at $65.

At most, the Catawbas could expect to receive a few cents per acre annually. For the life of their leases, the Catawbas and their descendants might collect a few hundred dollars, but payments often were not made in cash. Leaseholders typically bartered horses, guns and even slaves for their rent payments—and in their dealings with other settlers. In 1808, for example, John B. Springs bought the lease for "the Indian Land place," which formerly belonged to the Meacham family, for "four slaves ... three plow creatures and two horses."

In contrast, the leaseholders placed a much higher price tag on the land—judging by the amount they charged to sell or sublease to other white settlers. In some cases, leaseholders who rented land for few cents an acre sold it to other white settlers for $10 an acre.

Over time, the value of the land increased as the state built new roads and ferries in the area and leaseholders improved the land with homes, barns, grist mills and other structures. For example, a 230-acre tract on the headwaters of Half Mile Creek was originally rented in 1785 to Matthew Neely for fifty cents a year for the first ten years and $5 a year for the next eighty-nine years ($450 for the life of the lease). The property was sold to Allen Jones Green in 1803 and then purchased by Cadwallader Jones in 1818 for $3,400— seven times the value of the lease. Two years earlier, Jones had paid $3,260 for 402 acres on the west side of the Catawba River.

In 1816 William Moore, who leased land from the Catawbas for as little as fifty

◄ Alexander Faris' frontier cabin, located on the Anne Springs Close Greenway north of Fort Mill, was one of hundreds of new homes built on Indian Land by settlers. Courtesy of The Herald

cents a year, paid Andrew Herron $3,600 for 370 acres—almost $10 an acre. The property, located "on the Big Hill near the Great Pond" on the east side of the river, was originally leased by the Catawbas to Thomas Spratt and indicated the location of an Indian village on the survey plat.

A 515-acre tract originally leased to Samuel Knox for ten dollars, three horses, and a rifle in 1785 was sold for $2,000 in 1811 by Knox's son-in-law, Alexander Candlish, to John Jackson. Jackson's brother had warned that it would be difficult to get clear title to the land, and Indian Commissioner Hugh White had refused to sign the lease to transfer it to Jackson. The sale was contested in 1819 by Knox's granddaughter, Mary Candlish Sutton, and her husband, Alexander Sutton, who argued that Knox had willed the land to Mary in 1794. In the ensuing lawsuit, the court sided with the granddaughter, holding that Knox's will, even though it was executed in North Carolina, took precedence over the agreement between Candlish and Jackson. Despite the uncertainty over the title, neighbors testified at the trial that the land was probably worth $4,000 to $5,000.[56]

The disparity between what the Catawbas were paid and what the white settlers were willing to pay came about partly because rent payments to the Indians were fixed by the original contract. An annual rent of "ten Spanish-milled dollars"

may have been a fair price in the late 1780s, but at that time the region was largely undeveloped and sparsely populated.

As demand for land was growing and land values were rising, the Catawbas were locked into leases originally signed by tribal Head Men two or three decades earlier. The leaseholders, in contrast, had no restrictions on selling the leases or entering into subleases with newcomers to the area, and many of them took full advantage of the opportunity.

After two generations under the state-sanctioned system, Catawba leases had become big business. Nearly all of the tribal land had been leased, and the leaseholders were beginning to tire of their landlords.

56) The $2,000 sale of 515 acres would mean that Candlish sold the land to Jackson for around $3.83 per acre. Undeveloped land in the same area as the original Candlish land in 2004 is being sold for $40,000 or more per acre according to Judy Pettus Hawkins, head of Hawkins Realty of Fort Mill.

Paid in Full: Two Horses, Ten Silver Dollars, a Rifle, and a Bay Mare

There was clearly horse-trading involved when Samuel Knox obtained the first state-sanctioned Indian lease for 4,500 acres on November 15, 1785.

Knox had had already paid three Catawba Indians in advance for the twenty-five year lease, signed by Colonel John Airs, Major Brown, Major John Thompson, Captain Squash and Pine Tree George "with the consent of General New River."

The agreement actually commenced in 1783 with the payment of "nine silver dollars" to Colonel Airs and "a black horse delivered to Tom Cross." In 1784 Knox gave "one black mare to said Indians" in 1784, then in July of 1785 "one rifle gun and one silver Dollar to Colonel Airs" and another Catawba [whose name is illegible], and finally "one bay mare" on October 15, 1785.

Unlike later leases with terms of ninety-nine years, the lease gave Knox and his descendants an option to extend the twenty-five term, allowing Knox's heirs to rent the property forever:

"… upon conditions of the sd Saml Knox's paying to us the sd Indian chiefs or our heirs, the sum of ten silver Dollars yearly after the expiration of the aforesd term, the sd Knox to have and to hold the aforesd land for his and his heirs proper use and behalf forever, or as long as he or his heirs may please to hold the same."

The availability of inexpensive land attracted hundreds of families to York and Lancaster counties, fueling the growth of towns such as Fort Mill, shown here in the early 1900s. Courtesy The White Homestead Archives.

Land-Hungry for Catawba Real Estate

The Catawbas' fertile reservation became the site of new homesteads for hundreds of families moving to the area from as far away as northern Ireland and Scotland. One such settler, John Evans, a Philadelphia hatter who arrived in the area in 1789, paid Joseph Moore 613 British pounds for 370 acres. Moore had leased the land from the Indians only three months earlier.

Many of the people who rented land from the Catawbas were actually absentee leaseholders such as Samuel Knox who lived in Mecklenburg County, North Carolina. Other leaseholders held widely separated parcels on both sides of the river and sold or subleased the land to newcomers such as Evans.

Between 1806 and 1839, Dr. William Moore and James Moore signed twelve leases and amassed 3,000 acres on both sides of the river. The two men signed two leases together and entered into individual leases for a wide range of property including a "ferry landing" on the east side of the river.

A name that appears fourteen times on leases between 1817 and 1831 was "Cadwallader Jones." He controlled more than 2,500 acres on the west side of the river including a gristmill and a stone quarry. Although he rented some parcels from the Catawbas for a little as $6 a year, he paid at least two white leaseholders more than $3,000 for leased land.

Chapter Six

T h e   N e w   T r e a t y

Over the first two decades of the 19th century, a noticeable change emerged in the attitudes of the white settlers toward their leases and the process of leaseholding. In legal documents, such as a leaseholder's last will and testament, the terminology used to describe ownership of the land shifted.

In the beginning, leaseholders referred to "my lease of land inside the Indian Boundary" or "my Indian lease." Over time, the wording often became "my land" with the word "lease" dropped altogether. "Indian Boundary," if used, was shortened to "I.B." While some leaseholders still recognized the Indians' ownership, others dropped references to the Indians altogether. Second- and third-generation heirs often inherited "my land" with no acknowledgment that the land still legally belonged to the Catawba Indians.

Over time, legal disputes over the sales of Indian leases became more common because there was no legal requirement to record the lease and any associated mortgage at the county courthouse. John Springs III, who campaigned for reform of the leasing system, learned about its shortcomings in 1822 when he paid Edmund Jennings and John Sitgreaves $3,500 in cash for an Indian lease of 642 acres. In the lawsuit and counter suit that resulted from the sale, Springs insisted that Jennings sold him the lease without revealing a $2,602 mortgage on the land from a previous leaseholder, Dr. Samuel Henderson.

Henderson had mortgaged the Indian lease from "John Robinson, Thomas G. Blewett & the Executors of William Pressly, dec'd." Under normal circumstance, a title search at the courthouse would have uncovered the mortgage, but leases were rarely recorded at the courthouse.[57]

The leasing system began to unravel in the 1830s. In 1828, a rumor spread through Indian Land that Lowcountry investors wanted to buy the Catawbas' rights to the land. While state leaders said they would never support such a plan, the leaseholders began petitioning the legislature in 1830 to bring the leasing system to an end. The legislature directed the governor in 1832 to appoint commissioners to negotiate a settlement with the Catawbas. The gover-

◄ Betsy Crawford Harris Estridge sits outside her log cabin on the Catawba Indian Reservation in the early 1900s. CCPP Archives

57) Bill 63, York District Equity Court, filed January 9, 1822.

43

nor appointed James H. Witherspoon, Sr., Robert G. Mills,[58] Bird M. Pearson, John L. Miller and John M. Doby. Only Miller and Doby actually lived in Catawba Indian Land. The commissioners met with the Catawbas on November 6, 1833, at their major village, Old Town, in the Kings Bottoms of Lancaster District with a "considerable number" of white settlers present. Everyone left the meeting dissatisfied.

The commissioners wrote that it was evident that "influence of some kind had been used to prejudice the Indians against any negotiation." The Catawbas clearly believed the negotiators were there to take their land and drive them from the state.

For the Catawbas, the only possible rescue was in the hands of state government, and the solution increasingly rested on the sale of the Catawba lands to the whites. Rather than make outright cash payment to the Indians, state and local leaders thought it best to provide a reasonable yearly stipend to each Catawba family. State-appointed agents would administer the program, doling out food, clothing and other necessities to keep the Indians from spending of the state's money on alcohol.

In a letter written by Indian Land's David Hutchison at the request of Governor James Hammond, the Indians were viewed as corrupted by the leasing system. After the Revolutionary War when the Catawba women and children returned from

Virginia, Hutchison wrote, the women focused on collecting rent instead of maintaining the fields and harvesting crops. According to Hutchison, they became as "indolent and intemperate as the men, and even more so. They spent their time traveling about collecting their rents and lying about still houses and grog shops."[59]

Governor Robert Y. Hayne asserted in 1833 that it was impossible for an Indian tribe to "flourish" when surrounded by whites. Other than the overuse of alcohol, Hayne did not blame the Indians. He stated that white settlers owed the Indians approximately $2,000 a year in rents but actually paid them less than a third of that amount. Instead of cash, white settlers were paying their rents in whiskey, old clothes and provisions, with the whites setting the value. Despite these abuses, Hayne added that the Catawbas were good citizens of the state:

"… the Indians have preserved great harmlessness of manners, and an unshaken honesty. They perpetrate no crimes among the whites, and so few among themselves, that though without judicial tribunals or criminal laws of any description, they get along harmoniously together."

Hayne's solution was to drop the rent system entirely, have the settlers pay taxes on the land, and distribute the tax money to the Indians. Thus, he would "interpose the State between the settlers and the Indians." The Indians would have more money, and the whites would have legal titles to

58) Robert Gill Mills represented Chester County in the State Legislature. Elected Superintendent of Public Works of S.C. Known as Major Mills. Died Feb 8, 1842 in his 56th year. Buried at Fishing Creek, Chester County.
59) Brown, p. 292

John Springs III's Twenty-Five Indian Leases

John Springs III (1782-1853) acquired more Indian land and more leases than any other white settler. From 1810 to 1838, John Springs III's name appeared on twenty-five leases for a total of 5,947 acres. Springs held on to almost all of the land including the original site of Springfield plantation, selling off only 548 acres.

Born in Lancaster County Indian Land, Springs moved across Sugar Creek to the Fort Mill area after he married and began acquiring leases from Catawbas and white leaseholders. With so much of his land at stake, Springs took every opportunity to question the leasing system and suggest ways to reform it. He was chosen in 1840 to serve on the commission charged with negotiating an end to the leasing system.

Springfield, built by John Springs III in 1806.

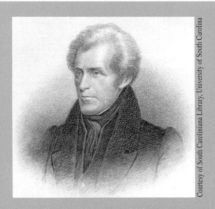

Courtesy of South Caroliniana Library, University of South Carolina

President Andrew Jackson's Ultimate Solution

The Catawbas' apprehension to negotiating with the state over the sale of their land is understandable. President Andrew Jackson had authorized the Indian Removal Act of 1830, following the recommendation of President James Monroe in his final address to Congress in 1825.

As a result of Jackson's ultimate solution for the "Indian problem," Cherokee Indians were driven from the Carolinas to Oklahoma on the Trail of Tears. The forced march through harsh conditions killed thousands of Cherokees and left many more living like renegades in the mountains of North Carolina.

For several decades, the westward push of whites had forewarned Indian tribes that some day they would lose their homeland. In the face of the state's intervention, the Catawbas probably feared they were powerless to stop it.

the land and be able to record them in the courthouse.

Following Governor Hayne's message to the state, the legislature appointed a committee to set up a program for buying the Catawba lands. A search for a copy of the 1763 treaty was unsuccessful, leading state officials to believe the treaty had never been recorded.[60] However, a plat of Catawba Indian Land was filed in the office of the Secretary of State and a certified copy was in the hands of Dr. John L. Miller, one of the commissioners, who had inherited it from his father.[61]

The legislature approached the Catawbas again in 1835 with Colonel J.S. Sitgreaves chairing a committee composed of Indian Land citizens Thomas Robertson, John M. Doby, and John L. Miller. Committee members reported they had "used their best exertions," but "from the dullness of comprehension or perverseness of two or three among them, we have been prevented in making a conclusive arrangement."

By 1835 most of the Catawbas had moved elsewhere, the majority of them settling among the Cherokee Indians. By that time, nearly all of their land was leased to the whites. More than 1,300 leases and subleases were recorded in Indian Commissioner Hugh White's book between 1785 and 1840. Several tracts were not yet leased, but since the Catawbas did not retain copies of the leases, it is doubtful

Courtesy of South Caroliniana Library, University of South Carolina

Governor Robert Y. Hayne

they were aware of these scattered holdings. The tribe owned 144,000 acres, but nearly 280,000 acres had changed hands through a dizzying number of transactions. In the last five years of the leaseholder system, from 1835 and 1840, White recorded more than three hundred transactions. Records indicate the tribe's land was running short. Many leases were signed for smaller parcels of fifty to sixty acres—some as small as two acres, as in the case of the lease to Catawba Baptist Church in 1837.

Gone were the days when a Catawba king was treated like royalty in the governor's manse. No longer were the Head Men attending Fourth of July celebrations and revered as heroes of the Revolution.[62] The few dispirited Catawbas who remained were not capable of dealing with white men

60) Actually there was a copy in the British Museum.
61) The plat, dated February 22, 1764, had been "done by the desire of Joseph Kershaw, February 7th, 1785."
62) General Jacob Ayers, the last Catawba to fight in the Revolution, was feeble by this time and died in 1837.

'Quite an Anomaly Under Our System'

In his 1833 address to the legislature, Governor Robert Y. Hayne described Catawba Indian Land as extremely fertile, embracing the best portions of York and Lancaster districts, populated by three thousand citizens "without one of them being the absolute proprietor of the soil." He described the Indian leaseholding as "quite an anomaly under our system" that was in need of reform:

"… the leases are readily sold to under tenants, for the full fee simple value of similar lands in other parts of the State, notwithstanding their liability to rents to the Indians … These lands are in a high state of cultivation, extensive improvements have been made upon them, and expensive buildings erected, and yet they pay no taxes to the State, and are held by better tenure than Indian leases, of which no record is kept, except in a small memorandum book of one of the Superintendents, liable at any time to be lost or mislaid. It cannot be desirable, either to the settlers or to the public, that this state of things should continue …"

who refused to pay rent or paid only with worn-out, unwanted goods.

In 1838 the legislature passed "An Act to Support the Catawba," which punished leaseholders who failed to pay their rents by requiring them to post a bond with the state treasury and pay a penalty of seven percent interest:

"… the lessee, or his or her heirs or representatives, shall execute to the State of South Carolina a bond, and lodge the same in the treasury of the upper division, which shall be a penal sum, the interest whereof shall be equal to the annual rent now payable by such lessee to the said Indians, and conditioned, that the said lessee shall pay annually into the treasury, on the first Monday in January, in each and every year, the interest of seven per cent, upon the said penalty, in lieu of the rent now payable by him, for the use of the said Indians; and in default of the punctual payment of such interest, the penalty of the said bond shall thereby be forfeited."

Between six hundred and seven hundred leaseholders were affected. Over the next year only seventeen leaseholders complied with the act—James Alderson, William Alderson, Thomas K. Cureton, Ann Garrison, James T. Henderson, John Henderson, David Hagins, John T. Hagins, Aaron Houston, Adam Ivy, Benjamin S. Massey, Allen Morrow, William Potts, Bela Sizer, James Stewart, James W. White, and T.S. Williamson. Almost all of them lived on the east side of the Catawba River with at least ten of the seventeen in the Lancaster District.

The massive show of resistance must have stunned the legislature. Yet, there is no record of any leaseholder being penalized. Instead, the reaction convinced the legislature that purchasing the Catawba lands was the best approach. On December 14, 1839, a resolution passed the House of Representatives asking Governor Patrick Noble to appoint five commissioners to meet with the Head Men of the Catawba tribe to buy the land.

The five commissioners chosen by the governor were John Springs III, David Hutchison, Edward Avery, Benjamin S. Massey, and Allen Morrow. None had previously served as commissioner, but each man was considered a community leader. Geographically, Hutchison and Avery lived on the west side of the river, Springs lived in the Fort Mill area and Massey and Morrow lived in Lancaster County. All five leased large tracts of land and were men "with whom the Indians were well acquainted and in whom they had confidence."[63]

Word was sent to the Catawbas in North Carolina and out West that the meeting would be held on March 13, 1840, at the crossroads of the Nation Ford road a mile from the west bank of the Catawba river.[64] All white men who leased land were invited. No one counted heads that day, but the following year 508 surveys of parcels were recorded by the state, with more trickling in over the next decade. No one knows how many Catawbas were present. The commissioners estimated the population of the tribe at eighty-eight people—twelve men, thirty-six women, and forty youths. Five Catawbas put their marks on the

63) Brown (quoted without attribution), p. 302
64) On July 30, 1960, members of the York County Historical Commission and the York County Historical Society met at Red River village on the lawn of the Randolph Yarns Mill to dedicate the Nation Ford Historical Park. Two markers were dedicated. One showed a large map of old roads and those existing in 1960. A second marker, contributed by the Southern Railway gave the history of the trestle and the ford. By 2004 there was no evidence of a park or the markers.

Photographed around 1855, Jesse Harris (1789-1873) moved from Virginia to Indian Land in Lancaster at the age of three.

treaty: General James Kegg, Colonel David Harris, Major John Joe, Captain William George, and Lieutenant Philip Kegg. Two white men represented two Catawba absentees—Sam Scott and Allen Harris.

With so many men gathered on the bank of the river, some historians have speculated that many jugs of whiskey were passed around that day, but it appears the negotiators were making a good faith offer to settle the matter. Articles two and three spelled out the terms:

"*Article Second. The commissioners on their part engage in behalf of the state to furnish the Catawba Indians with a tract of land of the value of $5,000.00, 300 acres of which is to be good arable lands fit for cultivation, to be purchased in Haywood County, North Carolina, or* in some other mountainous or thinly populated regions, where the said Indians may desire, and if no such tract can be procured to their satisfaction, they shall be entitled to receive the foregoing amount in cash from the state.

Article Third. The commissioners further engage that the state shall pay the said Catawba Indians $2,500 at or immediately after the time of their removal, and $1,500 each year thereafter, for the space of nine years …*"

News of the treaty was met by criticism from members of the state legislature, who feared "the settlers on Indian Land had cheated the Indians and swindled them out of their possessions." At the urging of Senator Isaac D. Witherspoon of York, commissioner David Hutchison wrote a defense of the treaty. The commissioners, he said, "tried to fix a sum, the yearly interest of which would be equal to the yearly rent secured in the leases. This we fixed at $21,000. It is not easy to ascertain with accuracy the amount of annual rents their lands have heretofore yielded. If the original survey is correct, their boundary contains 225 sections, which at ten dollars each, would produce $2,250." Hutchison reported that if the commissioners had agreed to pay everything in cash at the signing of the treaty, "they might have effected a treaty for one-third or even one-fourth of the amount."[65]

The legislature confirmed the Treaty of Nation Ford, and the tribe forfeited its rights to the land forever—although nearly all of the tribe's land had been leased through the early 1900s. To finance the treaty, the state levied a tax on the former leaseholders "of one cent and a half per acre" to repay the state. To obtain title to their land, the leaseholders were instructed to survey their land and submit the surveys with a lease or a tax receipt from the previous year to the Secretary of State.

Most of the leaseholders sent only their tax receipts, and the state transferred the titles into their names.[66] The leaseholder era was over, but the South Carolina never lived up to the promises made in the Treaty of Nation Ford. Although South Carolina would provide annual payments to the tribe through the next century, it never purchased the 5,000 acres of land in North Carolina or anywhere else.

The state of North Carolina refused to sell any land in Haywood County. Governor John M. Morehead wrote, in essence, that he knew South Carolina would never accept North Carolina's Indians, so he found no reason for North Carolina to accept the Catawbas. Besides, the few remaining Catawbas were not much inclined to leave the area.

Even though the treaty was never fulfilled, the governor, the legislature and area landowners probably considered the Catawbas' claim to 144,000 acres finally resolved in 1840. They could not have been more wrong.

---

65) Brown, p. 316.
66) Of the more than 600 leaseholders, only 128 returned copies of the leases.

Catawba Indians such as John Brown, shown here with his family in the early 1900s, worked small farms and cut timber on the tribe's 630-acre reservation.

Chapter Seven

The Land Claim

*T*he state's failure to secure land in North Carolina for the Catawbas under the terms of the Treaty of Nation Ford meant that South Carolina must find land valued at $5,000 for the tribe. Joseph F. White of Fort Mill was given the task of locating suitable land. He tried to buy land on the west side of the Catawba River on Big Allison Creek and failed.[67]

Most of the Catawbas had moved to Cherokee Indian territory but they were not welcomed there. Gradually the Catawbas drifted back to their old town sites. In his Reminiscences of York District, Maurice Moore described them as they passed through Yorkville: "… and they came back to the haunts of their forefathers, a living monument to the cupidity of the whites,

which must excite the sympathy of every generous heart."

Some Catawbas went West, mainly to Oklahoma and Arkansas, and in most cases did not return. Ten years after the treaty was signed, census figures identified only fifty-four Catawbas in South Carolina and fifty-six in North Carolina.

The favored spot for the returning Catawbas was the Kings Bottoms in the Indian Land community of Lancaster District. The bottoms were now in the hands of John M. Doby, but Doby refused to sell. In 1842 his brother, William Doby, was persuaded to sell 630 acres on the west side of the river. The steep slope of the land and periodic flooding made the land rocky and infertile. The state paid $6 per acre for land

it had purchased two years before for 15 cents an acre.

The few Catawbas who remained in the area were drifters living in tents and performing sporadic day labor, or they subsisted on the kindness of white neighbors. In 1870, Joseph F. White described their predicament to Lyman Draper of the Wisconsin Historical Commission:

"There is at this time about 80 head, they have a reservation of 600 acres of land, they think their condition is about as good as they could wish. I was well acquainted with them from my earliest days when they counted some 3 or 400; disipation has thinned them down to 80 head great & small."[68]

---

67) Brown, p. 319.
68) Draper MSS, Sumter Papers, 15 VV, p. 96.

The state withheld the initial payment of $2,500 to the Catawbas because the tribe never moved to Haywood County, North Carolina. The state also delayed the annual payments of $1,500. In 1849, Governor Whitemarsh T. Seabrook acknowledged the state's debt to the Catawbas was "about $18,000," which included 7 percent interest on the delinquent amount. Seabrook vowed that the state would pay the debt "and shall allow an interest of 6 percent payable annually, and said interest shall be divided in annuities per capita among the Catawba Indians."

The leaseholders completed their special tax payments in 1854 when the legislature released them "from the payment of any further sum or sums of money on account of advances made by the State to the said Catawba Indians."[69] The state continued to make payments to the Catawbas over the next century, except during the Civil War. Dr. Thomas Blumer of the Library of Congress estimated that the state's appropriations through the 1940s totaled $385,922.09, although it is impossible to determine how much was actually distributed to the tribe.

State agents were appointed to look after the Catawbas' welfare. By 1939 the state was appropriating $8,250 a year for the tribe. An agent, who was paid $450 annually, disbursed money and medicine for families and care of the aged. Despite the assistance, visitors to the reservation without exception reported dire poverty and corn crops destroyed by river flooding. Worst of all, the original forest was gone, leaving the Indians with no firewood for heating and cooking.

Throughout this prolonged period of poverty, many Catawbas held firmly to their faith in the tribe's land claim. As early as 1847, Catawbas living in North Carolina wrote the president of the United States, describing how they had been deprived of their ancestral lands and expressing their desire to "go west in one body." In 1848, Catawba Chief William Morrison wrote President James Knox Polk about the appointment of Samuel P. Sherrill as "our agent in the recovery of our claims against the state of South Carolina and to remove us west, having been badly treated, cheated, and defrauded by persons who acted as agent for us before Mr. Sherrill's appointment."[70] The letter to Polk, who had grown up less than five miles from Catawba Indian Land in neighboring North Carolina, "shows that soon after the Treaty of 1840, the Catawbas began to believe that they had a claim against the state … though they did not press their claim, the legend of it passed from generation to generation." The Polk administration could have questioned the legality of the treaty under the Non-Intercourse Act, which required all Indian treaties to be ratified by the federal government, but no one did.[71]

In 1848 and again in 1854, Congress appropriated $5,000 to "assist the (Catawbas) to emigrate and to sustain and settle them … among some of the tribes West of the Mississippi River." However, the money was never spent because the Chickasaws and Choctaws refused to allow the Catawbas to settle among them.

The Catawbas would appeal to the federal government for aid many times over the next century, but federal officials either failed to act or advised them to join Western tribes.[72] In November 1887, General James Kegg of the Catawba Nation wrote Secretary of Interior L.L.C. Lamar in Washington, seeking federal assistance obtaining a settlement of the tribe's claim. Kegg said he had been informed "the Federal Government had no control or jurisdiction" over the state's treaty with the Catawbas."[73] In 1895, the tribe submitted its "Petition and Memorial in the Matter of Claims and Demands of the Catawba Indian Association."

Despite the Catawbas' requests for aid, the federal government never appointed an agent to oversee the tribe.[74] In the federal government's eyes, the state of South Carolina had authorized the leasing system and was the only governmental entity that could exercise jurisdiction over the tribe. The attitude of the federal government was "we don't need to adopt any more Indians."[75]

69) Act 4180, Statutes At Large, Section II. 70) Brown, pp. 322-324.
71) Testimony of Congressman John M. Spratt Jr., Select Committee on Indian Affairs, U.S. Senate, July 22, 1993.
72) Journal of the House of Representatives of the General Assembly of the State of South Carolina, 1908, p. 282.
73) Ibid, p. 283. 74) Ibid, pp. 284-85.
75) Testimony of Congressman John M. Spratt Jr., Select Committee on Indian Affairs, U.S. Senate, July 22, 1993.

In December 1905, the Catawbas hired two attorneys, William F. Partlow and Chester Howe of Washington, D.C. to make the case that the Nation Ford Treaty of 1840 had not been ratified by Congress under the provisions of the Non-Intercourse Act. Partlow asserted the state owed the Catawba Indians the value of their lands, which he estimated to be approximately $2 million.[76] Partlow, a specialist in cases involving Indian affairs, vowed to the take the case to the U.S. Supreme Court.[77]

The U.S. Department of Interior declined to bring suit on behalf of the Catawbas because they were "state" Indians. The federal government once again advised the tribe to take its complaint to the state. In response, Governor Duncan C. Heyward asked Assistant Attorney General M. P. DeBruhl to examine the claim and prepare a history of the state's relations with the Catawbas. DeBruhl concluded that the Treaty of Nation Ford was valid because the Catawbas were "state" Indians with no standing under the Non-Intercourse Act. His lengthy analysis of the Catawbas' interactions with the state and federal government was submitted to Governor Heyward, who forwarded it to the House of Representatives. DeBruhl's last two pages included a list of the sums of money annually allotted to the Catawbas.

He noted that while the state had never paid the Indians the sum of $21,000

CCPP Archives

Chief Samuel Blue stands on the steps of the Church of Jesus Christ of Latter Day Saints in 1938.

within the time frame promised in the Nation Ford Treaty, the state had appropriated $27,000 for the Catawbas between 1841 and 1859. The House never debated the question but simply instructed the report to be printed in the House Journal in 1907.[78] A year later, the Catawbas again petitioned the Department of the Interior, but once again they were denied on the grounds that

Public Education and Rights for Catawbas

The first attempt to educate and "Christianize" the Catawba Indians came in 1803 through the efforts of the Rev. John Rooker, founder of Flint Hill Baptist Church, which established a missionary school near Sugar Creek. Initially, school teacher James Lewis gave sponsors some hope for success, but after several years the Indian children "became inattentive and the school was discontinued and the preaching was afterwards given up."

Nearly a century later, Mormon missionaries who had been run out of Rock Hill by whites, were welcomed on the Catawba reservation. The Church of Jesus Christ of Latter-Day Saints established a school there in 1898. Many Catawbas attribute the survival of the tribe to the intervention of the Mormons, who exemplified a strong work ethic and an aversion to use of alcohol.

The Catawbas were considered wards of the state, not citizens. They had a hard time finding jobs at local mills, and they did not have the right to vote or attend public schools in Rock Hill. Years later, the school district refused to send school buses to the reservation because the Catawbas didn't pay property taxes.

Under an agreement proposed by U.S. Senator James F. Byrnes, the tribe became federally recognized in 1943, and South Carolina agreed to let the Catawba children ride the buses and grant state citizenship to tribal members beginning in 1944.

76) The Record (Rock Hill, S.C.), December 14, 1905.
77) Ibid, February 19 1906.
78) Journal of the House of Representatives, pp. 286-87.

Aug. 15, 1912

A GROUP OF CATAWBA INDIANS.   INDIAN NATION NEAR ROCK HILL, S. C.

Pottery, made by the women and children in Catawba families, was an important source of income that enabled families to survive hard economic conditions.

no relationship existed between the federal government and the tribe. The U.S. Indian Service initiated its own investigation of the claim in 1910 and advised the tribe to pursue its claim against the state. Once again, the legislature declined responsibility for the tribe.

In 1924, the Catawbas submitted proposed legislation to the governor and legislature that would have given each tribal member twenty-five acres of land, a house with at least four rooms, farm equipment, livestock, and $100 per year for five years. In a letter to the legislature, Governor Thomas G. McLeod acknowledged that "a proper and satisfactory settlement of our relationship with the Catawba Indians has long been a problem in South Carolina." McLeod expressed his approval for the settlement, "which originated with the Business Men's Evangelistic Club of Rock Hill."[79]

The bill failed to pass, but the tribe was still pursuing a settlement in 1929 when Chief Samuel T. Blue wrote the federal commissioner of Indian Affairs:

We are still wards of the state and have been receiving an annuity at about $40 per head. I am kindly asking your office to inform me as to how you are settling with the Indians on different reservations. Do you give the certain amount of land with houses per head or two a family? Do you include stock and farm implements or give them so much money? If you would give me an outline of this question will be greatly appreciated. So should the state make settlement with my tribe I will have an idea what to look for.

Beginning in 1930, the State of South Carolina made a series of attempts to transfer responsibility for the welfare of the Catawba Indian Nation to the federal government. In 1936, the legislature budgeted $100,000 for the settlement of the claim, provided the federal government assumed responsibility for the welfare of the tribe. The appropriation went unused because no agreement could be reached with Washington. The next year, Dr. Frank Speck, an anthropologist with the University of Pennsylvania who documented the tribe's language and culture, wrote to the commissioner of Indian Affairs, asking for advice on whether the proposed settlement was fair.

Speck's letter prompted a visit to Rock Hill by the commissioner's administrative assistant, D'Arcy McNickle, who wrote a lengthy report about the Catawbas that laid the basis for an agreement between the state and federal governments. In 1937, U.S. Representative James P. Richards sponsored legislation to authorize the Secretary of the Interior to provide federal assistance. Richards' bill did not pass.

It would take six more years for Congress to agree to the Memorandum of Understanding (MOU). Under the memorandum, the Catawbas became qualified to receive federal assistance. The state agreed to pay $75,000 to buy more land for the tribe and $9,500 annually in 1944, 1945, and 1946 to be spent by the federal Farm Security Administration to help the Catawbas establish farms.

The Office of Indian Affairs agreed to provide $7,500 annually to support the Catawba Indian Association. In exchange, the state granted the Catawbas state citizenship, bought 3,434 acres of land near the reservation, and conveyed the land to the federal government. The state also was seeking the "release and quitclaim of all claims and actions, of whatsoever nature, against the State of South Carolina," but the wording was deleted from the final version of the memorandum on the advice of Fowler Harper, solicitor of the Department of the Interior.

The agreement was supposed to revitalize the tribe through farming on the expanded reservation. Assistant Commissioner Ward Shepard said he hoped "the tribe can become not only self-supporting, but can become a credit to the state." In time, however, the Catawbas became dissatisfied with the negligible services and benefits provided by the federal government. The government helped the Catawbas establish farms on the expanded reservation, but individual tribal members were unable to own the farmland.

In the post-World War II Baby Boom economy, many of the Catawbas became

79) Select Committee on Indian Affairs, U.S. Senate, July 22, 1993.

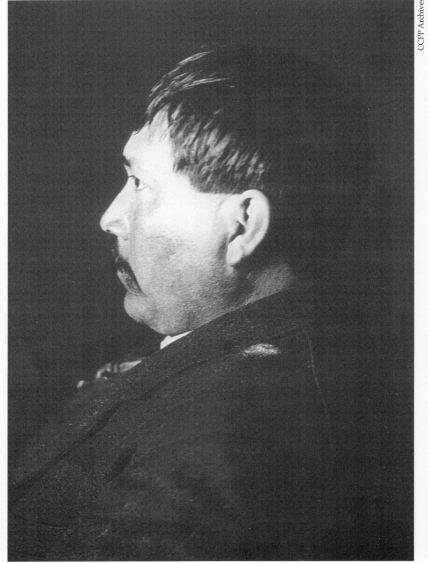

As members of the Catawba tribe, such as Mary Starnes and David R. Harris, earned the right to public education and access to local jobs, they began to want more opportunities for their children.

frustrated that they lacked titles to their land and could not obtain home mortgages. At the same time, the federal government's Indian policy shifted. In 1953, under House Concurrent Resolution 108, the government adopted the policy of terminating any special status tribe's had under federal law. After Congressman Robert W. Hemphill met with the tribe in 1959, the Catawbas agreed to termination of the relationship with the federal government but requested "an equitable distribution of the tribal assets." In Hemphill's resolution, the tribe also insisted, "nothing in this legislation shall affect the status of any claim against the state." Raymond A. Bitney, the Bureau of Indian Affairs agent assigned to work with the Catawbas, assured the tribe that termination would not impair their claim. However, some tribal council members were skeptical and strongly opposed termination. Bitney's report to the bureau was redrafted "to delete any controversial statements" and the original report was retained in a confidential file. It was apparent that the Bureau of Indian Affairs wanted to conceal any controversy over the status of the claim from relevant Congressional committees.[80]

The subsequent legislation, referred to as the Catawba Termination Act, was signed into law by President Dwight D. Eisenhower that same year. Section 5 of the act, which stated "the laws of the several states shall apply to (the Catawbas) in the

Boxes of Stolen Files for the Native American Rights Fund

Don Miller was a young attorney only three years out of law school in 1975 when he first met with members of the Catawba Indian Nation, and they handed him boxes of stolen federal files.

It is believed the files were copied by members of the American Indian Movement during their occupation of the Bureau of Indian Affairs for several days in 1973. The Catawbas knew only that someone called late one night to arrange a meeting to drop off the files.

Miller, lead attorney for the Native American Rights Fund (NARF), said the boxes of files were a great help. "Once we looked at those records and reviewed the history of the claim, we said, 'Yep, you boys definitely have a case,'" Miller recalled.

Over seventeen years, the Native American Rights Fund invested about 16,000 hours, mostly Miller's time, on the Catawba claim. The tribe's legal team was awarded about $5 million in legal fees from the $50 million settlement. NARF's proceeds went into a fund for fighting the legal battles of other tribes. For Don Miller, the Catawba land claim was a career-defining case that took him all the way to the U.S. Supreme Court.

When Miller paid his first visit to the Catawba Reservation, Miller had a one-year-old back at home. By the time the case was settled, the oldest of his three children was nineteen and stood six-feet, four-inches tall. "I didn't know anything could take this long," said Miller, a Missouri native who began his career in a legal aid office in Pueblo, Colorado. "What does a kid three years out of law school know?"[82]

80) Select Committee on Indian Affairs, U.S. Senate, July 22, 1993.
82) Cal Harrison, "Key Players: Profiles of Attorneys," The Herald, October 27, 1993.

same manner they apply to other persons or citizens within their jurisdiction," would handicap the tribe's pursuit of its claim two decades later. The Catawbas were not represented by counsel, and no one at the Bureau of Indian Affairs advised them that they must file suit on the land claim within ten years under South Carolina's statute of limitations. Even though tribal members expressed anxiety about their land claim, the bureau "never offered to help develop and document the claim, never offered the tribe legal advice about the validity of the claim, and never informed the tribe how to assert or adjudicate the claim."[81]

On July 1, 1962, the tribe's constitution was revoked and the termination process was completed. The 3,434 acres held in trust by the Secretary of the Interior were partitioned partly in kind among members of the tribe and partly by liquidation, with the proceeds distributed among the members of the tribe on a pro-rata basis.

Almost immediately, members of the Catawba community feared the tribe had lost something vital. The Catawba people would not survive without their tribal identity, and some feared they would lose all claim to their ancestral lands.

By the 1970s, younger members of the tribe were getting more involved in an effort to carry on tribal traditions such as pottery making and self-government. American Indians in the western United States were organizing and publicizing their plight of poverty and lack of proper health and educational resources. Militant Indian groups clashed violently with authorities in the name of "tribal nationalism" at places such as Wounded Knee, South Dakota, where two Indians were killed in a seventy-one day standoff.

The restoration of the Catawbas' claim began with a poker game in Maine. One of the card players bet a tourist cabin in the north of Maine and lost. The winner soon found himself in a boundary dispute with the Passamaquoddy tribe. To support the tribe's position, an old Indian woman came forth with a box of maps and papers that had been kept under her bed for years. The papers came to the attention of a summer intern named Tom Tureen. He borrowed the papers and started a lengthy study. Months later, at a tribal meeting, Tureen informed a gathering of incredulous Indians that they had a claim to much of the state of Maine.

The Passamaquoddy took their case to the Department of the Interior and asked Interior to sue the State of Maine. Interior refused to act on the ground that the Non-Intercourse Act applied only to federally recognized tribes. Interior had made the same argument to the Catawbas in 1907. But this time, the Passamaquoddy sued on their own; and in 1975, the First Circuit Court of Appeals sided with the Passamaquoddy. The court held that the Indian Non-Intercourse Act applied to all tribally held land. Soon, not only the Passamaquoddy and Penobscot, but also the Oneida in New York, the Narragansett in Rhode Island and the Mashpee in Massachusetts brought suit on their ancestral land claims.

In the same year, the Catawbas formed a non-profit corporation, the Catawba Indian Tribe of South Carolina, Inc., to participate in programs such as the Comprehensive Employment and Training Act, one concession the tribe retained under the Catawba Termination Act. A five-member executive committee was elected to oversee the corporation, and Gilbert Blue was elected chief. In June 1975, the Catawbas' executive committee authorized Chief Blue to contact the Native American Rights Fund, a non-profit group based in Boulder, Colorado that had been involved in numerous tribal land claims.

In the summer of 1976, Don Miller, an attorney with the Native American Rights Fund, met with the executive committee and told them that the Catawbas had a claim under the Non-Intercourse Act, one strong enough to be sued upon. The state of South Carolina had never submitted the Treaty of Nation Ford to Congress for ratification, and even if it had, the treaty would have been turned down for various reasons, among them the fact that South Carolina had had never fulfilled its promises, in particular its promise to spend $5,000

81) Select Committee on Indian Affairs, U.S. Senate, July 22, 1993.

for a new reservation. Joining the Native American Rights Fund would be a team of South Carolina attorneys, which over the course of the case included Robert Jones of Rock Hill and Jay Bender and Jean Toal of Columbia.[84]

The Solicitor of the Department of the Interior, Leo M. Krulitz, advised the department in 1976 that the Catawba Termination Act "did not abrogate the Secretary's responsibility to aid the tribe in the assertion of its claim." Therefore, the Interior Department asked the Department of Justice in 1977 to consider suing on behalf of the Catawbas. Attorney General Griffin Bell and Interior Secretary Cecil Andrus declined, recommending instead that "the administration should make an omnibus proposal to Congress to settle these claims."

Before federal officials could meet with the tribe, a split developed between tribal members who wanted per capita cash payments and members who wanted all settlement payments to go to the tribe. The faction seeking cash payments obtained a temporary restraining order against negotiations. The dispute was resolved by the appointment of a joint negotiating committee.

On June 30, 1978, Attorney General Bell advised Secretary Andrus that he would not bring suit in New York, South Carolina, and Louisiana. Bell wrote that he had "a number of questions about the legal and factual issues in these suits and question whether they can be won. Furthermore, the fact that the landowners are completely innocent of any wrongdoing weighs heavily against suing them."[83] While declining to sue, Bell suggested that Congress ratify the old treaties with "appropriate" compensation, determined either by Congress or the Court of Claims.

In reaction to the Catawbas' threat of a lawsuit, local landowners formed the Tri-County Landowners Association and hired lawyers of their own. Congressman Ken Holland had met with the Catawbas before his election and promised to help settle their claim. He intervened and tried unsuccessfully to negotiate a settlement.

A Catawba Claim Study Commission, headed by Representative Robert McFadden, D-Rock Hill, was formed to recommend a course of action. The commission recommended that the tribe receive $30 million, an expanded reservation, and federal and state services. But on October 27, 1980, the McFadden Commission came to an impasse, primarily over the size of the expanded reservation. A subcommittee had recommended the government buy up to 4,200 acres from willing sellers, but the full commission rejected this proposal by a vote of 4-3. Representative McFadden, Senator Don Rushing, and Godfrey Nims supported the proposal. Senator Coleman Poag, Representative Tom Mangum, George W. Dunlap, and Oliver Nisbet opposed the proposal.

The vote dashed any chances of settling South Carolina's largest lawsuit out of court. On October 28, 1980, the day after the Catawba Claim Study Commission rejected the terms of settlement, the Catawba Indian Tribe of South Carolina, Inc., then numbering about 1,200 members, filed a federal class-action lawsuit against 76 named defendants representing an estimated 27,000 landowners in York, Lancaster and Chester counties.

The named defendants included the counties of York and Lancaster and the city of Rock Hill; corporations such as Bowater, Springs, Duke Power, and the Southern Railway; Heritage Village Church and Missionary Fellowship, Inc. better known as PTL; and individual landowners, such as the Spratt and Close families of Fort Mill, direct descendants of two substantial leaseholders, Thomas "Kanawha" Spratt and John Springs III.

83) Select Committee on Indian Affairs, U.S. Senate, July 22, 1993.
84) Columbia lawyer Jean H. Toal, who served seven terms in the state House of Representatives, withdrew from the Catawba case in 1988 after becoming the first woman elected to the South Carolina Supreme Court. She would later become the state's first female chief justice.

Chapter Eight

The Settlement

The Catawbas never believed their lawsuit would win back possession of the original 225 square miles, which encompasses the cities of Rock Hill, Fort Mill and Tega Cay. However, the tribe sought monetary damages equal to the value of their land and "trespass damages" for more than 140 years, plus lost rents and profits, and attorneys' fees and court costs, all to drive home the gravity of their case. Because the lawsuit affected mortgage lending and the availability of title insurance, homeowners and business owners alike took notice.

The landowners' lawyers initially planned to fight the Catawbas' suit step by step, starting with a challenge to certification of the defendants as a class. The Hale and Dorr lawyers convinced them to put this issue aside and move to dismiss the suit. So, in June 1981, the defendants moved to dismiss, contending (1) that as a result of the "Catawba Termination Act," the Catawbas were no longer an Indian tribe within the meaning of the Non-Intercourse Act, and thus were unable to sue; (2) that state law now applied to the Catawbas, and state statutes of limitation barred their land claim; and (3) that the Treaty of Nation Ford was in effect ratified by the Catawba Division of Assets Act.

The motion to dismiss came before Judge Joseph P. Willson, a 79-year old judge from Pittsburgh, who was assigned the Catawba case when all the federal judges in South Carolina disqualified themselves to avoid any conflict of interest. On oral argument, it quickly became clear that Judge Willson was leaning toward the landowners. The landowners were relieved when Willson dismissed the Catawbas' lawsuit on all the grounds asserted in the motion to dismiss. But their victory was short-lived. The tribe appealed to the Fourth Circuit Court of Appeals, and in 1983, the Fourth Circuit reversed the lower court and held, "Clearly, Congress did not intend the Division of Assets Act … to end the Tribe's existence." Furthermore, the court of appeals ruled that the Supremacy Clause of the Constitution "preempted state law defenses, such as adverse possession or statutes of limitation," which require lawsuits to be filed in a timely manner.[85]

◀ Zachary Plyler enjoys activities at the Catawba's annual Yap Ye Iswe Festival in 1999. CCPP Archives

85) Select Committee on Indian Affairs, U.S. Senate, July 22, 1993.

Now the defendants appealed, taking the case to the U.S. Supreme Court. In 1986, the Supreme Court held that the state's statute of limitations did apply to the Catawbas, and while the Catawba Termination Act did not affect the status of the claim, "the Tribe thereafter had an obligation to assert its claim in a timely manner as would any citizen." The Supreme Court sent the case back to the Fourth Circuit Court of Appeals, saying that it was in a better position to determine the application of South Carolina real property law.

The court of appeals examined various state statutes imposing time limitations and ruled that state law barred the tribe's claim to any lands that were adversely possessed by the same party for ten consecutive years between the date of the termination, July 1, 1962, and the date the lawsuit was filed, October 28, 1980. The court then sent the case back to the district court.

The named defendants began moving for summary judgment by the district court, and the court released more than a thousand parcels and twenty-nine defendants from the lawsuit. The Catawbas appealed each such release to the Fourth Circuit, and then moved the District Court to act on their long-delayed motion for certification of the defendants as a class representing all landowners similarly situated. In 1991, Judge Willson rebuffed the Catawbas again by declining to certify the defendant class.

His decision meant that the tribe now had to sue thousands of individual landowners in the claim area.

The tribe appealed this ruling, but to no avail. So, on May 20, 1992, Chief Gilbert Blue announced that the tribe's lawyers were preparing complaints to be served on some 62,500 landowners in the claim area. Although he reassured property owners, saying they should not fear losing their land, documents called lis pendens were to be filed against every affected title in the three county courthouses, giving notice of the Catawbas' claim to any potential buyer or mortgage lender. While a large number of the landowners would be able to have the claim dismissed on the ground that they had "adversely possessed" their land for ten years between 1962 and 1980, a torrent of lawsuits would choke the courts. Congressman John M. Spratt Jr. called it "the legal equivalent of Hurricane Hugo."

As the litigation went on and on, the Catawba claim hung like a storm cloud over the claim area. No one knows for sure the actual impact the land claim had on the local economy. The city of Rock Hill and Fort Mill Township continued to grow. The resort community of Tega Cay, the Heritage USA Christian retreat of Jim and Tammy Bakker, and Carowinds Theme Park were all extensions of Charlotte, North Carolina, and all kept expanding. State and county officials, nevertheless, cited abundant anec-

dotal evidence that the claim was dampening industrial and commercial development. One developer lost dearly when his tract was rejected for what would become the largest shopping center in York County.

The Catawba claim was a particular challenge when foreign prospects were being courted. Daimler-Benz, a German automaker, considered York County as a site for a new assembly plant. A French insulation parts manufacturer, Sediver, selected an industrial park near York, because it was west of the claim area. County officials were told that to executives in France, the Catawba claim conjured images of feuding cowboys and Indians.

Faced with the economic impact, local government leaders grew more and more supportive of a settlement. Settlement talks had been abandoned when the lawsuit was filed in 1980. Until the law of the case was resolved and each side could determine the merits of the claim against available defenses, settlement negotiations hung in abeyance. After the Fourth Circuit Court of Appeals ruled on state law, it was apparent to the tribe that its case was substantially weakened, and it was apparent to the defendants that the lawsuit would not be completely dismissed on summary judgment.

In January 1989, defense counsel met with Congressman Spratt in Washington and asked him to use his "good offices" to restart the settlement negotiations. Spratt met with representatives of the Native American Rights Fund, Department of the Interior, the House Interior staff, the York County Legislative Delegation and the governor's office. He sent a background memorandum on the claim and a proposal for negotiations to Governor Carroll Campbell. In September of that year Governor Campbell, his executive assistant, Warren Tompkins, State Tax Commissioner Crawford Clarkson, Spratt's legislative counsel, Tom Kahn, and Spratt's district administrator, Robert Hopkins, met at the Governor's Mansion. Senator John C. Hayes, a long-time supporter of settlement, took part in the meeting, representing the legislative delegation.

Governor Campbell and Congressman Spratt decided to first approach Secretary of the Interior Manuel Lujan. After their meeting in January 1990, Lujan agreed that the Interior Department should be involved and that Interior should support some substantial part of the cost of settlement. A series of negotiations with the Catawbas took place over the next two years. Representing the Catawbas constantly were Chief Blue and Don Miller of the Native American Rights Fund (NARF), along with local counsel, Jay Bender of Columbia and Bob Jones of Rock Hill. Assistant Chief Fred Sanders and Secretary-Treasurer Carson Blue often joined in the negotiations, as did the Catawba Executive Committee: Dewey

Catawba Chief Gilbert Blue and Congressman John M. Spratt Jr. Courtesy of The Herald / Andy Burriss

Adams, Claude Ayers, Foxx Ayers, Buck George, and Wilford Harris.

The tribe opened the bidding with an offer to settle for $125 million. In June 1991, Congressman Spratt and Governor Campbell countered with an offer of $37.5 million. The counter-offer included the right to expand the reservation by up to 2,500 acres; the application of state laws on the reservation; a provision for tribal courts; tax exemption of reservation lands; a tribal sales tax equal to the local sales taxes; and

gambling rights limited to a special bingo license. The Catawbas rejected the offer and countered with a figure that was roughly double the amount.

On appeal of the district court's class action decision, oral arguments were heard in the Fourth Circuit Court of Appeals on February 4, 1992, and they did not go well for the Catawbas. The Catawbas lowered their counter-offer but continued to seek greater autonomy on the reservation, including gambling rights comparable to the Indian Gaming Regulatory Act, which had paved the way for tribal-run casinos on Indian reservations across the country.

When the Fourth Circuit allowed the district's court's decision against class action status to stand, the tribe announced it would forge ahead and sue more than 62,000 landowners individually. By NARF's calculation, the Catawbas had to file suit against the unnamed defendants by October 19, 1992, or run out of time. Congressman Spratt met with the Justice Department and sought the help of Senators Hollings and Thurmond. With their assistance, a law was moved quickly through Congress that suspended the running of time on the case until October 1, 1993, giving negotiators time to reach a settlement.

Later, when the negotiators met at the Catawba Community Center on the reservation, Congressman Spratt asked Chief Blue to take a walk with him to the river. As they walked, Spratt told Blue that $50 million was as much as he could reasonably hope to raise, but that if the tribe would agree to settlement at this level, he would endeavor to raise it; and the sooner the case was settled, the sooner federal recognition would bring in millions more in grants and benefits. Spratt and Blue informally agreed to shoot for a settlement in this range.

To allow time to work out the details of settlement, the tribe's attorneys set a deadline of October 22, 1992. After a straight week of negotiations, an agreement in principle was reached in the early morning hours of October 29, and the full tribe met later that day to approve it.

The negotiators still had details to resolve, including the role of the Indian Gaming Regulatory Act. The proliferation of video poker machines was a bitter issue in South Carolina, and the state did not want to empower the tribe to operate gambling halls. Most of the Catawba leaders were Mormon and personally did not like gambling, but felt they had a fiduciary duty to protect the tribe's rights to engage in a business that was making millions of dollars for other tribes.

By this time, the Catawba land claim was big news across the Carolinas, with reports surfacing on every twist of the negotiations. Despite progress, a headline in The Herald of Rock Hill proclaimed on December 31, 1992: "No End in Sight for Catawba Land Claim" as the suit "drags into its twelfth year." The next month, as Spratt recalled, negotiations resumed and after five days of negotiations ended with what was essentially the final agreement:

"The negotiations were intense, spirited, and sometimes contentious, as I have said, but they were conducted in the utmost good faith on all sides. Every element of the Agreement in Principle was negotiated in depth and detail. The Catawbas were represented throughout the negotiations."[86]

On February 29, 1993, Catawba tribal members met in Rock Hill and voted to accept the settlement worked out by the negotiating team. The Catawba Indian Tribe of South Carolina Land Claims Settlement Act of 1993 was passed by Congress and signed into law by President Bill Clinton in October 1993, and a similar law was passed by the South Carolina General Assembly.

Under the settlement, the Catawbas received $50 million over five years from federal, state and local taxpayers, as well as private sources. Almost two-thirds of the settlement was funded by the federal government, which contributed $32 million. In his testimony before the Senate Select Committee on Indian Affairs, Spratt made a strong case for Congress to pay the lion's share of the settlement. Spratt told the committee that from 1782, when the Catawbas first petitioned Congress for protection from intruders, to the Interior Department's failure to support the tribe's claim in the 1970s, the federal government had ignored more than twenty requests by the Catawbas for intervention.

"The federal government should bear a substantial part of the settlement because its derelictions have cost the tribe dearly. Had the federal government on any of the foregoing occasions upheld its trust responsibilities or carried out its contracts with the tribe, expressed or implied, the Catawbas would not have been denied redress for one hundred and fifty years

86) Select Committee on Indian Affairs, U.S. Senate, July 22, 1993.

Governor Carroll Campbell signs the Catawba Indian Tribe of South Carolina Land Claims Settlement Act as Congressman John Spratt, Chief Gilbert Blue, Foxx Ayers and other tribal representatives watch. Courtesy of The Herald

or lost the greater part of their claim by adverse possession. Their land claim would have been settled years ago by those responsible for it. Although the tribe's claim against the federal government has been barred by the statute of limitations, no law relieves the federal government of moral responsibility. Indeed, the government should be the last to hide behind the statute of limitations; for as Justice Hugo Black said, 'Great countries, like great men, should keep their word.'[87]

Under the settlement, the state's contribution was $12.5 million. The contributions from York and Lancaster Counties came to nearly $2.6 million. The balance was paid by title insurance companies, with whom Rep. Spratt negotiated a $1.4 million settlement, after he persuaded Duke Power and the City of Tega Cay to threaten suit. For its part, Duke Power Company offered $500,000 if matched by other private donations. Rep. Spratt and Robert Hopkins, his District Administrator, formed a committee, and with the help of Wayne Patrick, publisher of The Herald, raised more than the required match from private sector firms in the area. Crescent Resources Inc. had paid $500,000 in escrow to secure the release of a tract, and these funds were allowed to count toward the settlement.

The settlement payments were placed in five trust funds held by the Secretary of the Interior for the purpose of land acquisition, economic development, education, elderly assistance, and per-capita payments to tribal members. Under the settlement, 15 percent of the settlement funds were to be divided among qualifying members of the tribe, and one-third of the state and private contributions were to be earmarked for education.

The tribe was permitted to buy up to 3,000 acres to expand its reservation. The tribe's powers of self-governance were restored, and tax-exempt status was guaranteed for the reservation. The tribe agreed to abide by state environment and health laws, but reserved the right to adopt its own laws on the reservation and establish a magistrate-level tribal court. The Indian Gaming Regulatory Act was not to apply to the Catawbas, but the state agreed to grant the tribe up to two special bingo licenses allow-

87) Select Committee on Indian Affairs, U.S. Senate, July 22, 1993.

Above Left: Catawba potter Nola Campbell demonstrates the art of hand-shaped pottery, using many of the same techniques that have been passed down through generations of tribal members. Photos courtesy of The Herald

64

ing gaming six days a week with jackpots of up to $100,000. A 10 percent state tax would be levied on gross receipts.

Within the first year, federal funds provided a housing grant of $4.8 million for sixty homes for low-income elderly tribal members. Gravel roads were paved. Wells and septic tanks were financed. The tribe built the Long House on the reservation to serve as a center of government services and the place for members to gather for the tribe's General Council. A craft shop, display area, meeting room and tribal archive was erected on the reservation, and additional acreage was purchased along the river near Interstate 77 for a future museum. The Catawbas also bought the old Rock Hill Mall and established a tribal-owned bingo hall. In 2004, the tribe was pursuing plans to establish a second high-stakes bingo hall under the provisions of the settlement—and threatening to sue the state unless it assisted the tribe in its efforts.

It took 153 years—about five generations—to correct the faults in the Treaty of Nation Ford. The ultimate outcome could have been different if only the governor of North Carolina had been willing to accept the Catawbas or the state had found a suitable place to resettle them. The Treaty of Nation Ford awarded $21,000 in land and cash payments to the Catawbas, or about 15 cents an acre for the tribe's land claim. In 1993, the claim would finally be settled for

Shaping the Future of Rock Hill and Fort Mill

In the early 1990s, downtown Rock Hill was almost deserted and uncertainty over the availability of title insurance was interfering with the expansion of businesses along Rock Hill's North Cherry Road, the site of Rock Hill Mall. Developers were planning to build a new mall, and the likely location was a few blocks north of the old mall.

When plans for the Rock Hill Galleria were unveiled, the new mall was to be located on land exempted from the claim farther south on Interstate 77 at Dave Lyle

Boulevard Extension—part of the expanded 3,400-acre reservation that had been sold off in 1963 as part of the Catawba Termination Act. The location of the new mall and other new businesses in the sparsely populated area helped create a third major business district in Rock Hill.

On Earth Day, April 20, 1994, hundreds of people gathered in Fort Mill Township for the dedication of the Anne Springs Close Greenway. The 2,300 acres of undeveloped tract was set aside as a park by Anne Close and other descendants of John Springs III. An influential figure in the leaseholder era, Springs had pieced together the land through a series of Indian leases over twenty-eight years. Anne Close's father, Colonel Elliott White Springs, bought the land from his cousins at the end of World War II to establish a dairy that could provide milk for the cafeterias in his textile mills.

The crescent-shaped greenway, which contains remnants of the old Nation Ford Road, includes a nature center, several lakes for fishing and thirty-two miles of hiking, bicycling and horse trails. Designed to serve as a buffer between the suburban growth of Charlotte, North Carolina and the small-town charm of Fort Mill, the greenway includes a walking trail that passes by the site of Webb's grist mill, from which Fort Mill got the second half of its name.

The Catawba Indian Nation bought the old Rock Hill Mall and established a high-stakes bingo operation there under the provisions of the 1993 settlement.

about $350 an acre. Adjusted for inflation, the treaty of 1840 would have been valued at $277,000 in 1993 dollars—or about one-half of 1 percent of the amount of the $50 million settlement.[88]

In 1840, South Carolina mistakenly thought it no longer needed to recognize the Catawbas as a sovereign nation. State leaders assumed the tribe, like the 144,000 acres it once controlled, had simply faded into the mosaic of families settling South Carolina's Upstate. As it turned out, the Catawbas stoically held on to their tribal identity long after their ancestral lands were gone.

Ironically, the same legal principles related to treaties and land ownership that hastened the Catawbas' decline in 1840

helped restore the tribe's legal authority in 1993. Federal recognition restored many of the same powers reserved to the tribe in 1763 by the royal governor when he pledged the Catawbas "shall not in any respect be molested by any of the King's subjects within the said lines."

In the span of a lifetime, Scots-Irish settlers arriving in York and Lancaster counties witnessed the leasing of a nation. Parcel by parcel, the Catawbas leased away their hunting land, river fords, farmland—even the source of clay used to make their prized pottery. Throughout the tribe's history, governors, congressmen, and federal officials promised to find ways to lift the Catawbas out of poverty. The state-sanctioned leasing

system was created for that very purpose, but it failed to bring prosperity to the tribe. Certainly, no one forced tribal members to lease their land to the settlers, but with few opportunities to earn a living through other means, the Catawbas eventually became dependent on the rent money for their survival.

Some of the leaseholders made matters worse by bartering their rent payments—or refusing to pay all together. Unlike traditional landlords, the Catawbas were in no position to evict delinquent tenants and squatters. They repeatedly appealed to the state legislature, Congress and the president of the United States, but for the most part, their petitions for protection went unanswered. With the signing of the Treaty of Nation Ford, the responsibility for supporting the Catawbas was essentially transferred from the leaseholders to the state of South Carolina. State and federal assistance over the next century and a half was minimal, and the tribe remained largely poor and uneducated, while generations of Catawbas grew up believing they had been cheated out of their land.

In the end, the Catawbas retained only a tiny fraction of their 144,000-acre reservation; but with a $50 million settlement and federal recognition, the state of South Carolina and the federal government finally rendered modest justice to the Catawbas.

88) Consumer Price Index statistics from Historical Statistics of the United States (USGPO, 1975), Statistical Abstracts of the United States, The Inflation Calculator, http://www.westegg.com/inflation.

Adair, James. History of the American Indians. Edited by Samuel Cole Williams. New York: Promontory Press, 1986

Bailey, N. Louise. Biographical Directory of the South Carolina House of Representatives, Vol. IV, 1791-1815. Columbia, S. C.: University of South Carolina Press, 1984.

Blumer, Thomas J. Bibliography of the Catawba. Metuchen, N. J.: The Scarecrow Press, Inc., 1987.

Brown, Douglas Summers. A City Without Cobwebs: A History of Rock Hill, South Carolina. Columbia: University of South Carolina Press, 1953.

The Catawba Indians: The People of the River. Columbia: University of South Carolina Press, 1966.

Byrd, William II. Histories of the Dividing Line Between Virginia and North Carolina. Raleigh: N. C. Historical Commission, 1929.

Centennial History of the Associate Reformed Presbyterian Church (1803-1903). Published by order of the Synod. Charleston: Walker, Evans & Cogswell, 1905.

Calendar of Virginia State Papers, Vol. 1. Richmond, Virginia: Superintendent of Public Printing, 1873.

Cooper, Thomas, Ed. The Statutes at Large of South Carolina, Vols. I-V. Columbia, 1837.

Crane, Verner W. The Southern Frontier, 1670-1732. Durham, N. C.: Duke University Press, 1928.

Drayton, John. A View of South Carolina as Respects her Natural and Civil Concerns. Charleston, 1802.

Garlington, J. C. Men of the Time, Sketches of Living Notables . . . ., Spartanburg, S. C., Garlington Publishing Co., 1902.

Gregorie, Anne King. Thomas Sumter. Columbia, S. C.: The R. L. Bryan Company, 1931.

Hauptman, Laurence M. Between Two Fires—American Indians in the Civil War. New York: Free Press Paperbacks, 1995.

Hicks, Theresa M., Editor, and Wes Taukchiray. South Carolina Indians, Indian Traders and Other Ethnic Connections Beginning in 1670. Published for Peppercorn Publications, Inc. by The Reprint Company, Publishers, Spartanburg, S. C., 1998.

Hoffman, Margaret M. Colony of North Carolina, 1735-1764, Abstracts of Land Patents, Vol. 1. Weldon, N. C.: The Roanoke News Company, 1982.

Holcomb, Brent H. Anson County, North Carolina: Deed Abstracts, 1749-1766, Abstracts of Wills & Estates, 1749-1795. Baltimore: Genealogical Publishing Co., Inc., 1980.

Hudson, Charles. Four Centuries of Southern Indians. Athens: University of Georgia Press, 1975. The Southeastern Indians. Nashville: The University of Tennessee Press, 1976.

Journals of the House of Representatives 1785-1786. Lark Emerson Adams, editor. Columbia, S. C.: University of South Carolina Press, 1979.

Journals of the House of Representatives 1787-1788. Michael E. Stevens, editor. Columbia, S. C.: University of South Carolina, 1981.

Journals of the House of Representatives 1792-1794. Michael E. Stevens, editor. Columbia, S. C.: University of South Carolina Press

Kirkland, Thomas J. and Kennedy, Robert M. Historic Camden: Part One, Colonial and Revolutionary. Columbia, S.C.: The State Co., 1905.

Lawson, John. A New Voyage to Carolina. Chapel Hill: The University of North Carolina, 1967.

Lawson, John, Gent. Lawson's History of North Carolina. Richmond: Garrett and Massie, 1952.

Mecklenburg County, North Carolina, Minutes of the Court of Common Pleas and Quarter Sessions, 1780-1800. Transcribed by Herman W. Ferguson, 1995. Privately printed.

Mecklenburg County, North Carolina, Minutes of the Court of Common Pleas and Quarter Sessions, Volume II: 1801-1820. Transcribed by Herman W. Ferguson, 1997. Privately printed.

Mendenhall, Samuel Brooks. History of Ebenezer Presbyterian Church Including a History of Ebenezer Academy and the Town of Ebenezer. Rock Hill, S. C.: Reynolds & Reynolds, 1985.

Meriwether, Robert L. The Expansion of South Carolina, 1729-1765. Kingsport, Tennessee: Southern Publishers, Inc, 1940.

Merrill, James H. The Indians' New World: Catawbas and Their Neighbors from European Contact through the Era of Removal. Chapel Hill: University of North Carolina Press, 1989.

Milling, Chapman J. RedCarolinians. Columbia: The University of South Carolina Press, 1969.

Mills, Robert. Statistics of South Carolina. Charleston, 1826.

Moore, Alexander. Biographical Directory of the South Carolina House of Representatives, Vol. V, 1816-1828. Columbia, S. C., South Carolina Department of Archives & History, 1992.

Pettus, Louise. The Waxhaws. Rock Hill, S. C.: Regal Graphics, 1993.

Pettus, Louise and Ron Chepesiuk. The Palmetto State—Stories from the Making of South Carolina. Orangeburg, S. C.: Sandlapper Publishing, Inc. 1991.

Salley, Alexander S. The Boundary Line Between North Carolina and South Carolina, Bulletins of the Historical Commission of South Carolina, No. 10. Columbia, S. C.: The State Company, 1929.

Schoolcraft, Henry R. Historical and Statistical Information Respecting the History, Condition and Prospects of the Indian Tribes of the United States. 6 vols. Philadelphia: Lippincott, Grambo & Co., 1851-1857.

Schmidt, Elizabeth Whitman. "Occupants of Catawba Indian Land of York District, South Carolina taken from York County Deed Books A B C D E F 1786-1807. The South Carolina Magazine of Ancestral Research (Spring 1995).

Silver, Timothy. A New Face on the Countryside: Indians, colonists, and slaves in South Atlantic forests, 1500-1800. New York: Cambridge University Press, 1990.

Statutes At Large of South Carolina, Edited, Under Authority of the Legislature by Thomas Cooper, M. D.—L.L.D. Volume Fifth. Columbia, S. C.: A. B. Johnston, Printer, 1839.

Tadman, Michael. Speculators and Slaves. Madison, Wisc.: University of Wisconsin Press, 1996.

Teal, Harvey S. and Robert J. Stets. South Carolina Postal History and Illustrated Catalog of Postmarks 1760-1860. Lake Oswego, OR, 1989.

Wallace, David Duncan. A Short History of South Carolina, 1520-1948. Columbia: The University of South Carolina Press, 1951.

Wells, Lawrence K. York County, South Carolina Minutes of the County Court 1786-1797. Brent H. Holcomb: Columbia, S.C., 1981.

Unpublished Materials

Brown, Douglas Summers. "Background Notes and Subject Bibliography for A History of the Catawba Indians." Part 1. Rock Hill, S. C. 1956.

Draper MSS, Thomas Sumter Papers. University of Wisconsin. University Microfilm.

Lancaster County, S.C. Old Deed Book B.

National Register of Historic Places Registration Form. Prepared by Paul Gettys, Senior Planner, Catawba Regional Planning Council, Rock Hill, S. C.

Spratt, Thomas Dryden. "Recollections of His Family," compiled by Zack Spratt, typescript, 1875.

Secretary of State Papers Pertaining to State Grants on Catawba Indian Lands. 1798-1853. South Carolina Department of Archives and History.

Springs, John III. Store Account Book of J & E Springs, 1806-1833. Family History Archives, White Homestead, Fort Mill, S. C.

_____. Day Book, 1811-1847. Family History Archives, White Homestead, Fort Mill, S.C.

York County Conveyance Book B, 1788-92.
York County Court of Common Pleas.
York County Estate Records, Book A, B, C, O.
York County Equity Court Papers.
York County Mesne Conveyance Books E, F., L, M.
York County Probate Judge-Real Estate Book, 1825-1840.
York County Probate Office Sales Book, Inventories, Appraisements.
York County Records of the Court of Equity.
York County Will Book G.

Date of Lease	Lessee & Location	No. of Acres
Mar 1785	Samuel Knox of Mecklenburg Co., NC (all land between the two branches of Steel Cr., York Co.)	4500
20 Jul 1785	John Johnston (a promise to pay Catawba Head Men 820 Spanish milled dollars with 410 Spanish milled dollars to be paid in trade)	___
-- Jul 1785	David Hutchison (W. side of Catawba River on Nation Ford Rd)	___
1 Sep 1785	William Potts of Mecklenburg Co., NC (for 44£ NC money, land on Six Mile Cr., adj. John King's "fishing road")	___
2 Oct 1785	Alexander Faires (E. side of Catawba R.; York Co.)	___
____ 1785	Matthew Neely (W. side of Catawba R., York Co.; inherited from father, Jackson Neely)	___
____ 1785	Abraham McCorkle (Near Liberty Hill on Nation Ford Road, W. side of Catawba R., York Co..)	___
____ 1785	Robert Neely (W. side of Catawba R., York Dist.; inherited from father, Jackson Neely)	___
6 Mar 1786	Thomas Neel & James Campbell (on McWhorter's Br. of Fishing Cr., W. side of Catawba R., York Co.)	102
____ 1786	David Hutchison, aged 18 (on Nation ford Rd., W. side of Catawba R., formerly John Hutchison's)	___
19 Mar 1787	George Smartt (both sides of Nation Ford Rd., on waters of Steel Cr., York Co.; inherited from his father Francis Smartt, who stated that he had paid rents of the leased land for 14 years)	___
12 Jun 1787	Alexander Candlish (E. side of Catawba R., on E. side of Steel Cr.; York Co.)	___
24 Sep 1787	John Chambers (on Camp Br., York Co.)	403
17 Oct 1787	Isaac Smith (on Rocky Br., York Co., originally surveyed by John McClenahan, 1757; SW side on Indian Boundary line)	615 3/4
27 Oct 1787	Joshua Sturgis (on the Spring Br. of the Catawba R., York Co.; willed one acre by father Daniel Sturgis on south end of Punch's Landing)	1
6 Nov 1787	Thomas Drennan (on banks of Catawba R., York Co.; yearly ten Spanish milled dollars or the same value in goods or chattels)	650
6 Nov 1787	John Drennan (Allison's Cr. & Catawba R., York Co. ; rent of ten Spanish dollars)	635
6 Nov 1787	James Robertson (W. side of Catawba R.. York Co.; original lease from Catawba Indians)	304
25 Dec 1787	Mary Spratt (E. side of Catawba R., York Co.	640
25 Dec 1787	Thomas Spratt (E. side of Catawba R., York Co.; "Road from Salisbury to Ninety Six," or Nation Ford Rd.)	4535
____ 1787	John Baxter, Sr. & John Sellers (on road to old trading post, on Half Mile Cr., W. side of Catawba R.)	245 1/2
22 Feb 1788	Humphrey Williams (S. side 4 Mile Cr. where McClanahan's Rd crosses the creek, York Co.; formerly Capt. George Pettus, ' annual rent of 1 Spanish milled dollar, due Nov. 1)	300
12 Feb 1788	Estate of John Sawyer, John Garrison, admin. (on Nathaniel Irwin's path, a mill pond, both sides of Steel Cr. York Co.; including a sawmill, a fourth part of a grist mill, and two copper stills)	300
26 Feb 1788	Robert McRee & Jonathan Sutton (on dividing ridge of Steel Cr. waters, E. side of Catawba R.; 10 Spanish milled dollars rent each year for 99 years)	329
28 Apr 1788	Nathan Orr, Andrew Alexander, Thomas Alexander, Elijah Alexander and Matthew Alexander of Mecklenburg Co., N. C., all heirs of estate of John Sawyer, John Garrison, execuotr (E. side of Catawba R., both sides of Steel Cr., York Co. adj. Richison's land)	300
17 Sep 1788	James Greer of Mecklenburg Co., NC (on Clems Br. & both sides of the Charleston Rd., known as Steel Cr. Rd., Lancaster Co,)	320
____ 1788	Moses Thompson	___
8 May 1789	Hannah Miller (by will of husband Stephen Miller, filed in York Co., 22 Dec. 1789)	___
15 Aug 1789	Robert Brown (on Dutchmans Cr., W. side of Catawba R., York Co.; originally leased by Alexander Faires in 1789)	100
__ Aug 1789	Alexander Faires (Dutchmans Cr., W. side of Catawba R., York Co.)	100
15 Aug 1789	Robert McClenahan (W. side of Catawba R., York Co.)	100
17 Aug 1789	Joseph Moore (W. side of Catawba R., York Co.; also 5 acres)	370
4 Sep 1789	Henry Creswell (on main br. of Wild Cat Cr., W. side of Catawba R. York Co.; yearly rent of 10 silver dollars on Nov. 1, annually)	384
22 Dec 1789	Hannah Miller, widow of Stephen Miller (W. side of Catawba R.; York Co. left in will)	___
24 Dec 1789	John Evans, Philadelphia hatter (W. side of Catawba R.; York Co. formerly Joseph Moore's; bought for 613£)	370
____ 1789	Andrew Townsend	200
5 May 1790	William Craig (formerly John Hart's)	___
10 Jul 1790	Samuel McClellan (W. side of Catawba R., York Co.)	___
1 Sep 1790	James Simrel (on waters of Allison Cr., York Co. W. end of tract formerly Joseph Simril & William Berry's; land originally surveyed in NC for Joseph Simrel in 1752)	173, 155
13 Sep 1790	Laughlin Burns	640
27 Sep 1790	Joseph Moore (100£ NC currency to John Harris)	200
28 Sep 1790	John McBride (formerly John Harris')	200
28 Sep 1790	William Kennedy & Joseph Moore of York (E. side of Indigo Br., W. side of Catawba R., York Co,.)	200
17 Oct 1790	John Kelliah & Robert Vernor (on Climers Br. & Steel Cr. Rd, Lancaster Co.; formerly James Greer's)	320

Date	Description	Acres
Oct 1790	Andrew Stephenson (N. side Taylor's Cr., E. side of Catawba R., York Co.; formerly Matthew Neely & Hugh Neely's)	286
ca 1790	Moses Bigger (on waters of Sugar Cr. , York Co. & the NC boundary line)	100
1790	William McMurray (original grant)	187
5 Apr 1791	Elizabeth Davis (on Steel Cr., E. side of Catawba R., joining George Pettus' land, York Co.; yearly rent of 10 Spanish milled dollars due November 1, annually)	492
21 Apr 1791	Elizabeth Davis, widow of Joseph Davis (on Steele Cr., E. side of Catawba R., York Co. ; formerly Capt George Pettus,' rent of 5 silver dollars due on Nov. 1, annually)	
1791? 1794?	Jesse Harris (on Catawba R. & Hurricane Br., Lancaster Co.)	381
27 Jan 1792	John Willson, dec., Sarah Willson, Joseph Steele & Elijah Willson, admrs (the lease of Indian land was valued at 50£)	
10 Jul 1792	John Baxter (E. side of Catawba R. York Co. ; formerly Capt. John Harris')	332
9 Sep 1792	Clark Ticer (in the fork of Sugar Cr. & Steele Cr., York Co.; paid James Richardson 500£ for lease)	
22 Sep 1792	John McElwain (part of 615 3/4 acres originally surveyed for Isaac Smith, 1757, on Rocky Br., York Co., "Indian line")	140
22 Nov 1792	David Hutchison (W. side of Catawba R., on Saluda Rd., at Liberty Hill to Half Mile Cr. York Co. ; formerly Capt. John Harris')	
1792	William Bleckley (York Co.; originally Alexander Faires,' "in consideration of 50£ and interest from 2 October 1785, to be paid unto Isaac Laney")	160
5 Jan 1793	Priscilla Miller (on 12 Mile Cr., Lancaster Co.; inherited lease from her father, originally Robert McKlehenny's)	109
7 Jan 1793	James Clifton (on 12 Mile Cr., Lancaster Co.; inherited lease from his father, originally Robert McKlehenny's)	162
13 Sep 1793	Laughlin Burns (10 Spanish milled dollars to be paid each 27 Feb.)	640
27 Sep 1793	Thomas Alexander and Elijah Alexander (on Steel Cr., E. side of Catawba R.)	302
17 Oct 1793	Laban Sturgis (on W. side of Catawba R.)	
23 Oct 1793	Samuel Mitchell & Alexander Witherspoon (on Steel Cr., E. side of Catawba R. York Co.; received from Thomas Alexander and Elijah Alexander with agreement to pay off notes and bond	302
17 Dec 1793	Robert Clenahan [McClenahan] (on Dutchman's Cr., W. side of Catawba R., York Co.; originally leased to Alexander Faires)	100
1793	Charles Polk (on Johnny's Town Br., E. side of Catawba R., York Co.)	
1793	Guy Wallace (on Muddy Cr., N. side of 12 Mile Cr. Lancaster Co.; formerly leased by Charles Miller and Margaret Miller)	172
8 Mar 1794	John Baxter, Sr. (E. side of Catawba R., York Co.)	50
9 May 1794	Alexander Campbell (W. side of Catawba R., York Co.)	640
6 Nov 1794	Planner Winget & Franney Winget, his wife (E. side of Catawba R., adj. to Mark Garrison, James Richardson, Alexander Haynes, Thomas McMiers, York Co.; formerly John Garrison, Jr's; originally Thomas Spratt's; Winget to pay 17£ 10 sh. 6 p. sterling to Thomas Spratt., Sr., recorded 8 Mar 1802)	140
1794	Thomas Thompson (W. side of Catawba R., York Co.; from estate of father, Thomas Thompson, Sr.)	160
1794	John Thompson (W. side of Catawba R., York Co.; from estate of father, Thomas Thompson, Sr.)	160
4 Feb 1795	Samuel Elliott, Jr. (E. side of Catawba R., adj. to Isaac Garrison and Mark Garrison, York Co; paid 50£ sterling to Thomas Spratt)	193
24 Aug 1795	Isaac Weathers (E. side of Catawba R., York Co.; at junction of Big Sugar Cr. & Little Sugar Cr.; Samuel Blankenship & Benjamin Weathers, chain bearers for surveyor James Matthews)	353
3 Dec 1795	Rev. Bryce Miller (on E. side of Sugar Cr., Lancaster Co.; formerly William Grimes')	940
1795	Charles Miller (Lancaster Co. near NC line, just north of Gen. Thomas Sumter's camp on Clems Br.)	775
6 Apr 1796	Sally New River, Catawba Queen (in Kings Bottoms, on White Oak Br., Lancaster Co.; original grant to "weomen and children of the tribe forever)	534
21 Sep 1796	Samuel Lowrie (:bound unto Alexander Eakins, Sr. for $2,000," and to give Eakins possession 1 Feb 1797 for term of 94 years)	334
1796	Margaret McCorkle, widow; James McCorkle, Abraham McCorkle, Jr., Stephen McCorkle, heirs of Abraham McCorkle (W. side of Catawba R., York Co.)	
9 Feb 1797	Robert Harris (in "Mulberry fields," E. side of Catawba R., York Co.)	
17 Nov 1797	Abdon Alexander (on Catawba R. above Sugar Cr., York Co. ; formerly Bryce Miller's)	300
7 Dec 1797	Heirs of Elizabeth Davis: John Lycan Davis, Andrew Davis, James Davis, Hester Davis,William Davis, Rebecca Davis, Elijah Davis, Mary Parks and Walter Davis, Jr. (on "Knox's Road to Meacham's mill," E. side of Catawba R., York Co.; formerly Joseph Davis')	246
12 May 1798	Sterling Harris & Andrew Herron (on Sugar Cr., York Co.; formerly Thomas Spratt's)	460
1798	Adam A. Springs (E. side of Catawba R. York Co.; formerly Thomas Spratt's)	257
1798	Adam A. Springs (E. side of Catawba R. York Co.; formerly _____ McCaferty's)	163
1798	Adam A. Springs (E. side of Catawba R. York Co.; formerly _____ Moore's)	140
Feb 1799	John Bigger, Sr. (W. side of Catawba R., York Co.)	300
20 Feb 1799	Thomas Roach (E. side of Catawba R., York Co.; originally to Thomas Spratt)	122
Feb 1799	Abraham Roach (W. side of Catawba R. at Nation Ford, York Co.; formerly John Bigger & Joseph Moore, admin. of John Bigger, Sr.'s estate)	30
11 Mar 1799	Rev. William Blackstock & John Harris, Sr. of Mecklenburg Co., NC (on Fuller's Cr., Sturgis ferry road, near Old Nation Ford, York Co.; including Blackstock's mill site)	
28 May 1799	William Barnett Elliott (E. side of Catawba R., York Co.; formerly Thomas Spratt, Sr.'s)	159
30 May 1799	Daniel Bartlett (E. side of Steel Cr., York Co.; also surveyed same date as Daniel Barckley; 145 acres appraised for estate 24 Jul 1823 as 143 acres)	261, 145
20 Aug 1799	Lewis Talbert ("a tract of land in Col. Hill's claim in the Indian boundary & the Indian Springs along the Indian line" on Dutchmans Cr., York Co.; survey not recorded until 7 Sep 1812)	221
1 Feb 1800	Alexander Eakins, Sr. (E. side of Catawba R.. York Dist.; formerly Samuel Lowrie's)	154

Date	Description	Amount
10 Mar 1800	Stratton Edwards & Allen Knight (Taylor's Cr., York Dist.; formerly Hugh Neely's, originally granted to Matthew Neely))	178
14 Mar 1800	John Merrit (E. side of Catawba R., York Dist.)	60
28 Apr 1800	Charles Moore (formerly Hugh Ticer's)	194
5 Sep 1800	Archibald Barron (W. side of Catawba R.; York Dist.; formerly Nancy McCaw's)	318
27 Nov 1800	Solomon Simpson (formerly Benjamin Garrison's)	189
31 Jan 1801	James Cole Alderson & Thomas Barnett (E. side of Catawba R. from "Glover's corner to Great Road," York Dist.; paid $705, formerly Plumer Winget's)	128
4 Feb 1801	George Julien (E. side of Catawba R., York Dist.; inherited from father, Jacob Julien)	104
12 Feb 1801	Alexander Scott (E. side of Catawa R., York Dist.)	250
25 Feb 1801	Abel Alexander (E. side of Catawba R.; originally leased to James Webb	100
12 Mar 1801	Edmond Harris (on Sugar Cr., YorkDist.; formerly William Williams')	460
13 Apr 1801	William McMurry	521
13 Apr 1801	William McMurry & Joshua Sturgis	415
8 May 1801	William Pettus, George Pettus & Stephen B. Pettus (E. side of Catawba R., York Dist.; inherited from the estate of their grandfather, Samuel Knox)	1562
___Jun 1801	Randolph Cheek (at mouth of Coopers Br. & head of Hurricane Br., Lancaster Dist.)	160
2 Oct 1801	John Harris (on Johnny's Town Br., E. side of Catawba R. York Dist.; formerly Charles Polk's , for 200 French milled dollaars)	1,446
10 Oct 1801	John Rooker (E. side of Catawba R., York Dist.)	116
10 Dec 1801	James Stewart of NC (N. side of Clems Br., Lancaster Dist.; formerly Simon Climer's)	70
___Jan 1802	Spell Kimbrell (fork of Mill Cr & Sugar Cr., an original lease of James Richardson)	____
18 Jan 1802	Cheek Smith (fork of Mill Cr. & Sugar Cr. York Dist.; formerly Henry Ticer's)	____
28 Jan 1802	Henry Ticer (fork of Mill Cr. & Sugar Cr. York Dist.; inherited from father Clark Ticer)	____
16 Mar 1802	Andrew Townsend (formerly Thomas Knox's)	200
16 Mar 1802	Daniel Bartlett (on Steel Cr.,, York Dist..; original lease to John Campbell of Mecklenburg Co., NC, sold to Bartlett for $340)	261
___May 1802	Thomas Simpson (of Fishing Cr., W. side of Catawba R.; York Dist.; formerly James Willson's)	____
8 Jun 1802	Archibald M'Neal (E. side of Catawba R., York Dist. .; formerly Thomas Spratt's, 86 years remaining on lease)	100
8 Jun 1802	Thomas Meek (E. side of Catawba R., York Dist.; formerly Thomas Spratt's)	100
8 Jun 1802	Archibald Meek (E. side of Catawba R.;York Dist..; formerly Thomas Spratt's)	100
13 Aug 1802	Robert Linn (on 6 Mile Cr., York Dist.)	202
19 Oct 1802	Thomas Knox (formerly Andrew Townsend's)	200
28 Dec 1802	Andrew Tippin (N. side of Taylor's Cr., York Dist.; formerly Andrew Stephenson's)	286
_____1802	James Faris, Richard Faris (E. side of Catawba R., York Dist.; heirs of James Faris)	____
_____1802	Rebecca Atkins, widow of Samuel Atkins (on 4 Mile Cr., near Nation Ford Rd, W. side of Catawba R., York Dist.)	____
_____1802	John Henderson Barry (on br. of Wild Cat Cr., W. side of Catawba R., York Dist.; formerly William Barry & friend John Barry, purchased from Samuel Creswell)	____
1802/1803	William Glover, James Barnes Glover, Mort--- Glover, John Glover (E. side of Catawba R., York Dist.; heirs of James Glover)	____
1802/1803	William Arnold ("1 peace of land from Catawbas; originally leased for $3.50 by Josephus Arnold)	74
1802/1803	John Bell, Robert Bell (E. side of Catawba R., York Dist.; heirs of Robert Bell)	____
20 Jan 1803	Thomas Knox (W. side of Catawba R.; York Dist; formerly Henry Fuqua's)	400
4 Mar 1803	James Spratt, Sr. (E. side of Catawba R., York Dist.)	390
2 Apr 1803	John Smyth (E. side of Catawba R., York Dist.; formerly Alsey Rogers')	127
2 Apr 1803	Charles Carroll (formerly Thomas Knox's)	160
16 Apr 1803	Samuel Wright (formerly Michael Henderson and Ann Steadman's, originally Henry Byrne's)	98
18 May 1809	Rev. William Blackstock (mill site, W. side of Catawba R., on Half Mile Cr., York Dist.)	11 1/2
21 Oct 1803	Allen Jones Green (on headwaters of Half Mile Cr., W. side of Catawba R., York Dist.; formerly Margaret "Peggy" Neely's)	237 1/2
_____1803	Robert Harris (Johnny's Town Br., E. side of Catawba R., York Dist.; formerly John Harris')	1,446
_____1803	Charles Sansing	
28 Jan 1804	Cheek Smith (on forks of Steel and Sugar Crs., E. side of Catawba R., York Dist. for $600 paid to Henry Ticer of Mecklenburg Co., NC. as agent of Robert Harris, executor of estate of Clark Ticer)	____
14 Feb 1804	Spring Hill Academy, James Harris, Esq. of York Dist. & William Patton of Mecklenburg Co., NC, trustees (E. of Catawba R., adj. to William McKinney, Alexander Scott & Elijah Davis; formerly Thomas Barnett's)	12 1/2
18 Feb 1804	James Fisher Gordon of Mecklenburg Co., NC (E. side of Catawba R.; formerly George Smart's & bought for $1,000)	
25 Feb 1804	Thomas Reid of Chester Co., merchant (formerly David Patton's)	140

5 May 1804	Samuel Craft (W. side of Catawba R., York Dist; formerly Jonathan Beaty's of Yorkville, "plantation James Clinton now lives on")	110
23 Jun 1804	Hugh White (W. side of Flaggy Br. on the old Mill road; formerly Thomas Spratt's)	530
23 Jun 1804	Thomas M'Neal (down the Flaggy Br. to Joseph White's corner upon the Stony Hill; formerly Thomas Spratt's)	____
19 Aug 1804	Andrew Kennedy (originally William Kennedy's; 75 years remaining)	100
11 Sep 1804	Thomas Reid of Chester Dist. (W. side of Catawba R.;. York Dist.; formerly David Patton's, sold for $95.04)	140
10 Nov 1804	Alexander Falconer ("whereon the Carters lived; formerly Thomas Harp's, sold for $210)	____
10 Nov 1804	James B. Fulton ("whereon Thomas Harp lived," sold for $600; William Edward Haynes, admin. of Harp's estate)	300
5 Dec 1804	Bailey & Waller, Charleston merchants (formerly Thomas Knox's, originally William McMurry's)	521
5 Dec 1804	Bailey & Waller, Charleston merchants (formerly Samuel McClellan's, originally Robert McClellan's)	95
5 Dec 1804	Bailey & Waller, Charleston merchants (on Tools Fork, W. side of Catawba R.; part of 640 acre tract formerly Andrew Creswell's)	262
____ 1804	Robert Lesley, guardian of Thos. Neel, minor (W. side of Catawba R.; lease bought with horse valued at $65)	365
____ 1804	Martha Elliott White & son William Elliott White (E. side of Catawba R., York Dist.; heirs of Capt. Joseph White)	____
7 Mar 1805	James Graham (E. side of Catawba R., York Dist.; originally Samuel Knox's)	131
25 Mar 1805	Samuel Anderson, William H. Anderson & John Anderson, Jr. (main branch of Wild Cat Cr., W. side of Catawba R.,York Dist.; formerly Henry Creswell's, sold for $1028)	384
24 May 1805	James Turner, Sr. & James Turner, Jr. (at Old Nation Ford, both sides of Saluda Rd. at Catawba R. York Dist.;formerly Moses Thompson's)	____
6 Jul 1805	John Tally (formerly William Kennedy's)	200
4 Aug 1805	James Currithers (on the W. bank of the Catawba R., York Dist.)	515
22 Oct 1805	Hugh White (E. side of Catawba R.; York Dist. formerly Thomas Spratt's)	____
22 Oct 1805	Abraham Roach (E. side of Catawba R., York Dist.; formerly Hugh White's)	____
____ 1805	Nancy Eakin, widow ("in Indian clame;" in will of Alexander Aiken/Eakin)	____
14 Jan 1806	William Moore & James Moore (formerly John Tally's)	200
27 Jun 1806	Dr.John Hemphill (formerly Buday W. Wheeler & James B. Fulton's)	187
30 Sep 1806	James B. Fulton	165
22 Aug 1807	Alfred R. Alexander (W. side of Catawba R, York Dist.)	185
23 Sep 1807	Sinthy Craig & Tirsy Craig, daughters of William Craig, dec'd by will of their uncle James Allen)	____
25 Dec 1807	Zebulon Jackson (both sides of Providence Rd., E. side of Catawba R., York Dist.; formerly Hugh White's, originally Thomas Spratt's)	530
____ 1807	Alexander Faires (on Old Camden Rd. near Half Mile Cr., W. side of Catawba R., York Dist.; survey by John McClanahan shows border with John Patton)	245
____ 1807	Isaac Garrison, Hugh White & Arthur Ervin (on Steel Cr. & Hagler's Br., E. side of Catawba R., York Dist.; received by will of Thomas Spratt, Sr. "said tract I allow to be equally divided betwixt Isaac Garrison, Hugh White and Arthur Ervin either by partition or sale as they think best.")	681
____ 1807	John Barnett (E. side of Catawba R., York Dist.; willed by father, John Barnett, Sr., "the plantation he now lives on," originally William Arnold's)	____
5 Jan 1808	Charles Miller (E. side of Catawba R., Lancaster Dist.)	320
10 Feb 1808	Matthew Marable and Richard Auton (E. side of Catawba R., York Dist.)	295 1/2
12 Feb 1808	John Harris	300
20 Apr 1808	Elias Garrison (on middle fork of Dutchman's Cr., W. side of Catawba R., York Dist.)	125
10 May 1808	Samuel Roach (on Wildcat Br. of Fishing Cr., York Dist.)	49
-- Jul 1808	Hugh White (E. side of Catawba R., York Dist.; originally Thomas Spratt's)	210, 141, 153
6 Sept 1808	Joshua Gordon (E. side of Six Mile Cr., Lancaster Dist.; near 12 Mile Cr. & mouth of Long Br.; original lease, rented for 7 years at $.50 per year and then for $13 for remainder of 99 year lease)	800
25 Sep 1808	Samuel Blue (at mouth of Coopers Br. & head of Hurricane Br., Lancaster Dist.; formerly Randolph Cheek's)	160
5 Dec 1808	John Parks (formerly Alexander Erwin's, inherited by Sarah Parks)	117 1/2
____ 1808	Robert Tilghman (E. side of Catawba R., York Dist.; original lease, for $1.00 per year for 99 years)	113
____ 1808	(E. side of Catawba R., York Dist.)	430
____ 1808	Sarah Patton, widow of Robert Patton (W. side of Catawba R., York Dist.; Robert Patton purchase from James Baxter)	____
____ 1808	Edmond Weathers (E. side of Catawba R., York Dist.)	147
____ 1808	Mary Smith (on Sugar Cr. and NC line, E. side of Catawba R., York Dist.; inherited from father John Dinkins)	100
____ 1808	James Graham (E. side of Catawba R., York Dist.; original lease, rent of $.50 for 99 years)	51
____ 1808	Fowler Williams (Belair Academy land, Lancaster Dist.)	____
____ 1808	Charles Robertson (W. side of Catawba R., York Dist.; formerly James Sansing's)	200
____ 1808	John B. Springs ("the Indian Land place;" formerly ____ Meacham's; bought for "4 slaves and three plow creatures, 2 horses")	____
20 Jan 1809	John Springs, Jr. (E. side of Catawba R., York Dist.; formerly William Parks')	46

Date	Description	Acres
2 Feb 1809	Arthur Erwin (E. side of Catawba R.)	295
6 Feb 1809	Frederick L. J. Pride (S. side Taylor's Cr.; formerly William Walker's)	47
17 Aug 1809	Nancy George (Catawba Indian)	80
21 May 1809	Joseph Daniel (on Pinckney Rd., York Dist. ; formerly David McCance's who designated 2 acres for the use of the congregation of Neely's Cr. Church)	611
_____ 1809	William Reeves admin. of estate of Allen Reeves (formerly Andrew Willson's)	400
2 Jan 1810	Robert Kimbrell (fork of Mill Cr. & Sugar Cr., York Dist.; formerly Cheek Smith's)	_____
20 Jan 1810	John Bennett (two tracts)	116
10 Feb 1810	Thomas Spratt, Jr. (on Catawba R.; originally leased to Thomas Spratt, Sr. who willed "my part of the ferry with 36 acres of land")	36
30 Mar 1810	William Moore (E. side of Catawba R.; originally James Moore's)	200
8 Jun 1810	John Springs, Jr. (E. side of Catawba R., York Dist.)	280
16 Jun 1810	John Wallace	175
1 Jul 1810	Alexander Candlish (E. side of Catawba R.; originally Samuel Knox's)	_____
3 Jul 1810	Spell Kimbrell (on W. side of Sugar Cr. across from McAlpine Cr., York Dist.)	165
8 July 1810	Henry Coltharp (W. side of Big Sugar Cr., E. side of Catawba R., York Dist.; an original lease, rented at $2.50 per year for 99 years)	83
13 Jul 1810	Richard Sadler (W.side of Catawba R.; part of it formerly Robert Meacham & William Erwin's)	280
18 Jul 1810	Richard Springs (E. side of Sugar Cr. & Clems Br., Lancaster Dist.; plat shows "old Indian Path," north of Clems Br.)	640
20 Jul 1810	Matthew Goodrich (E. side of Catawba R., York Dist.; annual rent of 50 cents for 8 years, then in 1818 to rent at $15 annually)	360
20 Jul 1810	George Wallace (E. side of Catawba R., York Dist.)	175
20 Jul 1810	Zebb Jackson (E. side of Catawba R., York Dist; originally leased to Thomas Spratt, formerly held by Thomas Roach)	122
20 Jul 1810	Daniel Davis (on Neelys Br. of Fishing Cr.; original lease, at $.50 per year until 1832 and then at $3.00 per year for the balance of 99 years)	300
20 Jul 1810	Richard Sadler (on main Fishing Cr.,York Dist.; $5.00 per year for 99 years)	150
20 Jul 1810	John Smith (E. side of steel Cr., York Dist.; formerly Daniel Bartlett's)	261
20 Jul 1810	John Springs III , Jr. (E. side of Catawba R. on Old Nation Ford R. and Webb's Mill Rd. York Dist.; original lands of Springfield plantation)	648
20 Jul 1810	John Springs, III (E. side of Catawba R., York Dist.)	280
21 Jul 1810	William Parks (on fork of Bennett's Spring Br. at mouth of Spratt's Br., E. side of Catawba R., York Dist.; $.50 per year for 28 years and then at $2.75 per year for balance of 99 years)	215
21 Jul 1810	Thomas Robertson (on Tools Fork of Fishing Cr., York Dist.; for $10.00 per year for 99 years)	250
21 Jul 1810	James Wilson (E. side of Catawba, York Dist.; formerly Spell Kimbrell's)	
21 Jul 1810	John Kimbrell & Solomon Kimbrell (E. side of Catawba R.;, York Dist.; from James Wilson on same day that Wilson received the lease from Spell Kimbrell)	_____
16 Aug 1810	Isam Shirling	545
17 Aug 1810	William Pettus (on NC line, includes Still House Br.), E. side of Catawba R.; York Dist.; rent of $.50 per year for 49 yearsand then at $10 a year for the balance of 99 years)	640
17 Aug 1810	Isaac Garrison (E. side of Catawba R., York Dist.)	683
17 Aug 1810	Joseph Laney	110
17 Aug 1810	Matt Marable (2 tracts of land: 101 1/2 & 154 acres, on E. side of Catawba R., York Dist.; surveyed for Marable and R. Auton, Feb 10, 1808)	295 1/2
18 Aug 1810	William H. Anderson & John Anderson (on Wildcat Br. "below the Still House of John Gallant, Esq.," W. side of Catawba R., York Dist.; $.50 per year for 20 years and then $4.50 for the balance of 99 years)	384
18 Aug 1810	William Wright (W. side of Catawba R., York Dist.; $.50 per year for 5 years and then $1.25 per year for the balance of 99 years)	112
18 Aug 1810	James Spratt (E. side of Catawba R., York Dist.)	875
18 Aug 1810	William Partlow (E. side of Catawba R., York Dist.)	96
20 Aug 1810	Hugh Ticer (fork of Mill Cr. & Sugar Cr., E. side of Catawba R., York Dist.; formerly Robert Kimbrell's, John Springs III, estate admin.)	_____
8 Sep 1810	Hezekiah Thorn, William Faires & Jonathan Neely (W. side of Catawba R., including mouth of India Hook Br., York Dist.; formerly Samuel Dinsmore's)	169 1/2
14 Sep 1810	Joshua Tilghman (E. side of White's Cr., "across the nobes of several hills," E. side of Catawba R., York Dist.; an original lease, rented for $.50 per year for nine years then at $3.00 for the balance of 99 years)	200
18 Sep 1810	William B. Elliott (E. side of Catawba R., York Dist.; originally to Thomas Spratt, surveyed Sept 29th 1810 by John McClenahan, rent $5)	159
18 Sep 1810	James Spratt (E. side of Catawba R., on both sides of Nation Ford Road, York Dist.)	875
28 Sep1810	James Spratt (E. side of Catawba R., York Dist.; surveyed by his father, James Spratt, Sr. on 4 Mar 1803)	320
28 Sep 1810	Hezekiah Thorn (White's Br., E. side of Catawba R., York Dist; rent of $.50 per year until 1815 and then $5.00 per year for the balance of 99 years)	380
28 Sep 1810	Hezekiah Thorn (on White's Br., E. side of Catawba R., York Dist.; $.50 per year to 1829 and then $5.00 for the balance of 99 years)	300
28 Sep 1810	William Partlow (on White's Br. & Jackson Spring Br.,.E. side of Catawba R., York Dist.; original lease, $2.50 per year for 99 years)	96
28 Sep 1810	Alexander Scott (E. side of Catawba R., York Dist.; surveyed 12 Feb 1807)	250
28 Sep 1810	James Currithers (S. side of Catawba R. York Dist.; surveyed 4 Aug 1805)	515
28 Sep 1810	Isaac Garrison (E. side of Catawba R., York Dist.)	683

29 Sep 1810	Hugh White (E. side of Catawba R., York Dist.)	53
29 Sep 1810	William Jackson (E. side of Catawba R., York Dist.; original lease rented at $2.50 per year for 99 years)	210
29 Sep 1810	Zebulon Jackson (E. side of Catawba R. on Camden Rd., containing Green Pond or Turkey Br. & 2 spring branches, York Dist.; $.50 rent per year to 1813 and then at %5.00 per year for the balance of 99 years)	530
2 Oct 1810	James Thomason (on E. side of Indigo Br., W. side of Catawba R., York Dist.; formerly William Moore's; $.50 rent per year for 6 years then at $1.50 per year for the balance of 99 years)	200
2 Nov 1810	John Ginnings (on Dutchman's Cr., W. side of Catawba R., York Dist.; Sarah Gilbreth, guardian)	75
____ 1810	William Moore (formerly James Moore's)	200
12 Mar 1811	William Turner Ingram (on Indian line and Granney's Rd., York Dist.; originally Joseph Cathcart's)	306 3/4
29 Mar 1811	John Jackson (E. side of Steel Cr., York Dist.; $2.000, formerly Alexander Candlish')	515
30 Mar 1811	Robert Saville (on W. side of Sugar Cr., E. side of Catawba R., York Dist.; original lease, $10.00 per year for 99 years)	510
28 Apr 1811	William Nivens (E. side of Tools Fork of Fishing Cr., W. side of Catawba R., York Dist.)	232
30 Apr 1811	Jeremiah Cheek (on Sugar Cr., Lancaster Dist.)	202
1 May 1811	Edmond Weathers (E. side of Catawba R., York Dist.)	261
1 May 1811	Samuel McWhorter Belew (E. side of Sugar Cr. at Hurricane Br. & mouth of Coopers Br., Lancaster Dist.)	124
1 May 1811	Joseph Hunter (on Clems Spring Br., Lancaster Dist.)	52
1 May 1811	Hugh White (on E. side of Catawba R. York Dist.; part of original lease to Thomas Spratt, Sr.)	210
1 May 1811	Charles Gillespie (on Sugar Cr., Lancaster Dist.)	131
1 May 1811	David Wilson (on W. bank of Catawba R. York Dist.; formerly John ' "including the mill and improvements formerly Allen Reeves, dec'd, Hance McWhorter surveyor with George Sturgis and Dudley Reeves, chainbearers)	365
14 May 1811	John S. Sitgreaves'minor children, John Sitgreaves, Allen Green Sitgreaves, & Amelia Sitgreaves, heirsof Halstead Davis, Est. (on 6 Mile Cr., York Dist.)	____
18 May 1811	Richard Parham	241
___ May 1811	Elizabeth Pettus Jackson, widow (E. side of Catawba R., York Dist.; formerly William Jackson's)	210
3 Jun 1811	James Darnell (on waters of Six Mile Cr., Lancaster Dist.; surveyed by William Wilson, John Crockett & Thomas Boyd, chainbearers)	100
4 Jun 1811	Richard Black (Lancaster Dist.)	100
4 Jun 1811	Daniel Smith	213
6 Jun 1811	Abraham Miller (E. side of Catawba R. on McAlpine Cr., Lancaster Dist.; original lease, rented for $1.30 per year for 99 years)	230
7 Jun 1811	Martha White, widow of Capt. Joseph White (E. side of Catawba R., York Dist.; plat shows 4 3/4 acres allotted to Unity Presbyterian Meeting House, formerly Thomas Spratt, Sr's)	126
7 Jun 1811	Samel Elliott (E. side of Catawba R. York Dist.; originally leased to John Garrison, Sr. and part originally leased to Thomas Spratt, Sr., plat shows "Meeting House" of Unity Presbyterian church)	134
7 Jun 1811	Robert Saville (on W. side of Sugar Cr., York Dist.)	510
7 Jun 1811	George Heskett (E. side of Sugar Cr., Lancaster Dist.)	157
7 Jun 1811	Samuel Elliott (E. side of Catawba R.; formerly Thomas Spratt, Sr's)	134
7 Jun 1811	Thomas Boyd (a resurvey on 3 Jun 1811)	200
7 Jun 1811	Henry Hartwell Glover (E. side of Catawba R., York Dist.; original lease, $2.50 per year rent for 99 years)	105
7 Jun 1811	Simon Climer (on Sugar Cr., Coopers Br., & Climers Spring Br., Lancaster Dist.)	170
7 Jun 1811	Thomas Black (E. side of Sugar Cr. & McAlpine Cr., Lancaster Dist.; original lease, $.50 per year for 99 years)	252
7 Jun 1811	Thomas Robertson (on Tools fork of Fishing Cr.,W. side of Catawba R., York Dist. ; $.50 rent for 21 yearsand then $10.00 per year until balance of 99 years)	364
7 Jun 1811	John M'Gill & Sarah M'Gill, admin. of Thomas. M'Gill, dec'd (W. side of Sugar Cr., York Dist.)	225
7 Jun 1811	Stephen Smith (E. side of Catawba R., including juncture of Webb's Mill Rd. & Camden Rd., York Dist.; originally Thomas Spratt, Sr's)	430
7 Jun 1811	James Darnell (E. side of Catawba R.; on waters of Six Mile Cr.; Lancaster Dist.)	100
7 Jun 1811	Drury Smith, assignee of John Rooker (E. side of Catawba R., York Dist.)	____
8 Jun 1811	Martha White for William E. White, a minor (E. side of Catawba R., on "Great Road to Webbs Mill;" York Dist.; $2.50 annual rent to Sally New River and $3.00 annual rent to Col. Jacob Ayres, both Catawbas, an original lease for 99 years)	350
11 Jun 1811	James Thomasson (W. side of Catawba R., York Dist.)	288
14 Jun 1811	James Thomasson (on Indigo Br., W. side of Catawba R., York Dist.)	125
9 Jul 1811	William P. Thomasson (W. side of Catawba R., York Dist.; original lease, $10.00 per year for 99 years)	288
16 Jul 1811	James Harris	100
17 Jul 1811	William McWatters (on Catawba R., York Dist; original lease to Charles Miller, formerly James Webb's)	320
17 Jul 1811	Richard Springs (E. side of Sugar Cr., Lancaster Dist.; original lease, rent of $1.00 per year for 99 years)	100
17 Jul 1811	John H. Hood (E. side of Sugar Cr., Lancaster Dist.)	77
17 Jul 1811	John Black (S. side of McAlpine Cr. at its juncture with Sugar Cr., Lancaster Dist., with "Old Indian path:" originally leased to Thomas Black	100

Date	Description	Acres
6 Aug 1811	Dr. Buckner Lanier (W. side of Sugar Cr., York Dist.)	332
6 Aug 1811	Dr. Buckner Lanier (Lancaster Dist.)	203 1/2
5 Aug 1811	William Amberson (on Watson Br., W. side of Catawba R., York Dist.; formerly David Sadler's, including 5 acres purchased from William McCorkle)	88
18 Aug 1811	Matthew Nickle (original survey for John Drennan)	73
18 Aug 1811	Drury Ashecraft (original lease, rented for $.25 per year for 10 years and then for $2.25 for the balance of 99 years)	249
21 Aug 1811	Nathaniel Harris (W. side of Sugar Cr., both sides of M'Gills Br, York Dist.)	314
21 Aug 1811	Henry Tally (on Sugar Cr. & White Oak Br.)	665
28 Aug 1811	Robert McCreight (on branch of Fishing Cr.; included 77 acres surveyed 18 Sep 1802 for David McRight, rented for $.50 per year for 10 years and then $1.50 for the balance of 99 years)	218
28 Aug 1811	William Rivers W. side of Catawba R., York Dist.; original lease, rented for $2.75 a year for 99 years)	202
28 Aug 1811	John Sides (W. side of Catawba R., York Dist.; original lease, rented at $.50 per year for 6 years, then at $1.50 per year for 99 years)	99
28 Aug 1811	Henry Sides (on Cane Run of Fishing Cr., W. side of Catawba R., York Dist.; original lease, rented at $.50 per year for 6 years, then at $1.50 for balance of 99 years)	88
29 Aug 1811	William Stewart (original lease, rented at $.50 per year for a term (not named) of years, then $5.00 per year for balance of 99 years)	320
30 Aug 1811	William Partlow (E. side of Catawba R., York Dist.; subleased from William Pettus for 98 years; rent of $1.25 yearly to be paid to William Pettus' sons:William Wadkins Pettus, Stephen Bullock Pettus & George Pettus)	——
___ Aug 1811	William Fuller (E. side of Catawba R., York Dist., on Joshua Tillman's mill pond; formerly WilliamPettus," originally Samuel Knox's)	100
6 Sep 1811	John Carroll (W. side of Catawba R., York Dist.; original lease, $.50 for 29 years, then $6.33 per year for the balance of 99 years)	524
14 Sep 1811	John Steel	160
17 Sep 1811	John Ashecroft (E. side of Cain Br. of Fishing Cr., York Dist.; original lease, rented at $.50 per year for 21 years, then at $4.00 per year for the balance of 99 years))	567
18 Sep 1811	Benjamin Patterson (on White Oak Br., E. side of Catawba R. , York Dist.)	204
18 Sep 1811	Benjamin Weathers (W. side of Sugar Cr., S. side of Little Sugar Cr. York Dist. ; surveyed for Isaac Weathers, 24 Aug 1795)	353
18 Sep 1811	Churchwell Anderson (on 12 Mile Cr., Lancaster Dist.)	144
18 Sep 1811	Churchwell Anderson (N. side of 12 Mile Cr. and W. side of 6 Mile Cr. Lancaster Dist.,. 2 wagon roads, one to bridge & one to ford of 12 Mile Cr.; original lease, rented for 99 years)	654
18 Sep 1811	Jesse Sledge (on 12 Mile Cr. & both sides of 6 Mile C., Lancaster Dist.,)	275
18 Sep 1811	James Morrow (both sides of Tar Kill Br., Lancaster Dist.; original lease, rented at $5.25 per year for 99 years))	429
18 Sep 1811	Richard Ross (E. side of Sugar Cr., both sides of Long Br., Lancaster Dist.)	255
18 Sep 1811	Andrew Rea (lying between NC line, Steel Cr. Rd., & Clems Br., Lancaster Dist.)	133
18 Sep 1811	Andrew King (E. side of 12 Mile Cr., Lancaster Dist.)	217
18 Sep 1811	John Moore (on Sugar Cr., Lancaster Dist.)	226
18 Sep 1811	Jeremiah Cheek (on Sugar Cr., Lancaster Dist.)	202
18 Sep 1811	John Steel (on Steel Cr. Rd., Lancaster Dist.)	160
18 Sep 1811	John Thompson (lying between Steel Cr. Rd. & NC line, Lancaster Dist.)	124
18 Sep 1811	William Dobie, Esq. (lying on Catawba R. & Sugar Cr., Lancaster Dist.)	222
18 Sep 1811	Agnes Crockett (E. side of Sugar Cr., Lancaster Dist.)	155
25 Sep 1811	James Harris (original lease, rented at $.50 per year for 12 years that at $3.50 for the balance of 99 years)	230
25 Sep 1811	Matthew Nickels (S. side of Dutchman's Cr., York Dist.; formerly John Drennan's)	73
26 Sep 1811	James Baxter (fomerly Andrew Townsend's & conveyed to him by Henry Carswell, John Carswell, Thomas Carswell & Robert Carswell; original lease, rented fir $1.00 per year for 99 years))	200
26 Sep 1811	James B. Glover (on Ductchman's Cr., W. side of Catawba R., York Dist.; original lease, rented $1.75 per year for 99 years)	115
26 Sep 1811	Allen Davis (lease later sold to Daniel Sturgis)	——
28 Sep 1811	James Spratt (on Old Nation Ford Road, E. side of Catawba R., York Dist.)	
___ Sep 1811	William Doby (W. side of Sugar Cr. near Doby's Bridge Rd., York Dist.; original lease, rented at $.50 per year for 6 years then at $10.00 for the balance of 99 years)	225
___ Sep 1811	James Miller (E. side of Sugar Cr., York Dist.; formerly William Crockett's & signed by Agnes Crockett, widow of William; Joseph Walkup & Robert Crockett, administrators)	155
2 Oct 1811	William McRee (E. side of Catawba R.; York Dist..; original lease to Robert McRee, dec'd)	320, 30
2 Oct 1811	James Spears (on Clems Br. & NC line, Lancaster Dist.; original lease, rented at $2.50 per year for 99 years)	70
2 Oct 1811	Jane Baxter, relict of (E. side of Catawba R.; originally leased by John Bigger, Sr. & surveyed for John Baxter, Sr., 18 Mar 1794)	150
2 Oct 1811	Hamilton Horn (on E. side of Catawba R.. York Dist.; originally leased to James Webb and formerly Abel Alexander's)	100
2 Oct 1811	John Harris (E. side of Steel Cr., York Dist.)	300
2 Oct 1811	John Culp (on Clems Br. & the Indian Road, Lancaster Dist., 3 tracts; original leases, rented at $.50 per year for 12 years and then at $5.00 per year for 99 years)	323.5
2 Oct 1811	Bartlett Meacham (E. side of Catawba R., York Dist; originally leased by Robert McRee)	97
2 Oct 1811	Wilson Weathers & William Weathers, heirs of Isham Weathers (E. side of Steel Cr., York Dist.; surveyed for Elsey Weathers)	128
2 Oct 1811	James Wilson (both sides of Dutchmans Cr. & on W. bank of Catawba R., York Dist.; originally leased to Benjamin Garrison)	280

Date	Description	Acres
6 Oct 1811	James Spears (Clems Br., Lancaster Dist.;. annual rent $2.50)	70
22 Oct 1811	William Alderson (E. side of Steel Cr., York Dist.; known as Jack Alderson place)	90
6 Dec 1811	James Powell	100
7 Dec 1811	JesseTyson	35
9 Dec 1811	James Webb Estate (E. side of Catawba R., York Dist.)	1,009
_____ 1811	Benjamin Patterson (on White Oak Br.; original lease, rented at $.50 per year for 9 years and then at $3.63 per year for the balance of 99 years)	204
_____ 1811	Elizabeth Pettus Jackson (E, side of Catawba R., York Dist.; inherited from husband, William Jackson)	210
_____ 1811	James Baxter (on Wild Cat Cr.,W.side of Catawba R., York Dist.)	353.5
31Jan 1812	FrederickL.J. Pride ("Penne Wood Place', W. side of Catawba R., York Dist.; original lease, rented at $6.00 per year for 99 years)	162
31 Jan 1812	Frederick L. J. Pride (W. side of Catawba R., York Dist.; original lease, rented at $.50 for 11 1/2 years and then at $4.25 per year for the balance of 99 years)	102
31 Jan1812	Joseph Steele & Mary Steele (formerly James Steele's)	97
20 Feb 1812	John Chambers	___
21 Mar 1812	Charles Gillespie (Lancaster Dist.)	181
23 Mar 1812	Joseph Moore	388
4 Jun 1812	James Harris Estate (W. side of Sugar Cr., York Dist.)	100
4 Jun 1812	A. Frew (W. side of Sugar Cr.; formerly James Harris' estate)	475
4 Jun 1812	John Springs III (on Steel Cr., York Dist.; with mill pond, originally surveyed for Arthur Erwin)	295
4 Jun 1812	Isham Sherling (W. side of Sugar Cr.; York Dist.)	545
4 Jun 1812	Eliakim Colvert (on Six Mile Cr., Lancaster Dist.)	135
14 Jun 1812	Eliakim Colvert (Lancaster Dist.)	192
18 Jun 1812	John Chambers (on Fishing Cr., W. side of Catawba R. York Dist.; original lease, rented at $.50 per yer for 18 years and then at $10.00 for the balance of 99 years)	560
18 Jun 1812	Samuel Robinson (on both sides of Six Mile Cr., Lancaster Dist.; formerly John Tutt's)	340
18 Jun 1812	Gray Westbrook & Robert Workman (on Fishing Cr.; W. side of Catawba R., York Dist.)	205
18 Jun 1812	John Moore (E. side of Sugar Cr., Lancaster Dist.,at Walter Miller's spring; original lease, rented at $.50 per year for 6 years and then at $5.50 per year for the balance of 99 years)	263
31 Jul 1812	Joseph Steele (W. side of Catawba R., York Dist.; original lease, rent of $1 per year for 99 years)	97
31 Jul 1812	Frederick L. G. Pride (W. side of Catawba R., York Dist.; original lease rented at $.50 per year for 10 years and then at $10.00 per year for the balance of 99 years)	___
6 Aug 1812	Isaac Parish (W. side of Catawba R., York Dist.; original lease, rented at $1.25 per year for 99 years)	200
6 Aug 1812	Isaac Parish (W. side of Catawba R., York Dist.; original lease, rented at $4.50 per year for 99 years)	567
6 Aug 1812	Susanna Blankenship (E. side of Catawba R.;York Dist.; originally leased to John Garrison, formerly Jesse Tyson's)	35
6 Aug 1812	Joseph Jackson (on E. & W. side of Hagler's Br., E. side of Catawba R.; York Dist.; lease called for rent of 50 cents per year for 10 years & then $3.50 per year for remainder to the end of 99 years)	240
10 Aug 1812	Josina Garrison (on W. side of Catawba R.)	86
10 Aug 1812	John Starr (millpond on Dutchmans Cr.; W. side of Catawba R.; part of Arthur Garrison's old survey)	06
17 Aug 1812	Zebulon Jackson (E. side of Catawba R., York Dist.)	402
26 Aug 1812	Alexander Faires (E. side of Catawba R., York Dist.)	744
26 Aug 1812	Jacob Jones (side of Dutchmans Cr., W. side of Catawba R., York Dist.; "all the swamp & bottom land to the edge of the hill or his high water mark, except the timber; formerly David Garrison & James Garrison's)	___
7 Sep 1812	Lewis Talbert (W. side of Catawba R., York Dist., original lease, rented for $4.00 per year for 99 years)	221
10 Sep 1812	John Gibbons (on McAlpine Cr., Lancaster Dist.; rented at $1.80 per year for 99 years, resurveyed by James Harris, Esq. In 1824 as 105 acres)	96.5
10 Sep 1812	Samuel Gibbons (on E. side of Sugar Cr., Lancaster Dist.)	103
10 Sep 1812	John Crawford (on E. side of Sugar Cr., Lancaster Dist.)	131
10 Sep 1812	James Spratt, Jr. (E. side of Catawba R.; York Dist.; originally granted to Robert McRee, surveyed by James Spratt, Sr.)	150
17 Sep 1812	Daniel Sturges (W. side of Catawba R., York Dist.; original lease, rented at $.50 per year for 24 years and then at $4.00 for the balance of 99 years	179
17 Dec 1812	John Starns (rented at $1.00 per year for 99 years)	86
20 Sep 1812	Thomas Gibbons (rented at $1.75 per year for 99 years)	105
21 Sep 1812	William Baxter (W. side of Catawba R. at ferry landing)	132
22 Sep 1812	Andrew Herron (York Dist.; original lease to John Bigger, rented for $.50 per year for 3 years then at $4.50 per year for the balance of 99 years	276
28 Sep 1812	Thomas Barnett (E. side of Catawba R., York Dist.; original lease to William Elliott, Sr.)	312
5 Nov 1812	James Harris (on Sugar Cr., York Dist.; formerly John Smith & Mary Smith's)	100
1 Dec 1812	John Springs (E. side of Catawba R., York Dist.; original lease to Nathaniel Irvin, Sr.)	208
21 Dec 1812	James Harris (E. side of Catawba R., York Dist.: original lease to Nathaniel Irvin, Sr.)	208

	Hugh Riddle (W. side of Catawba R., York Dist.; originally William Howe's)	106
2 Feb 1813	John McCulloch (Lancaster Dist.; formerly Robert Crockett's)	345
13 Feb 1813	William Smiley Hamilton (SE side of Cain Run, York Dist.)	51
3 Apr 1813	John Baxter (on E. side of Catawba R.; resurvey)	643
4 May 1813	James Powell (W. side of Steel Cr., S. side of Spratt's Br.; formerly J. Jackson's, rented at $1.25 per year for 99 years)	100
4 May 1813	John Smith (E. side of Catawba R., York Dist.)	100
4 May 1813	George Givens (transferred from James Powell, same day)	100
4 May 1813	Thomas Barnett (E. side of Steel Cr., York Dist.; originally leased to William Elliott, Sr., rent of $1.00 annually for 99 years)	162
4 May 1813	Benjamin Dunlap (on Six Mile Cr., York Dist.; rented at $.50 a year for 5 years and then at $10.00 annually for the balance of 99 years)	635
4 May 1813	William Moore (E. side of Catawba R., York Dist.; originally Thomas Spratt's)	276
4 May 1813	John Bennett (York Dist., 2 tracts, 70 acres on E. side of Steel Cr. & 45 1/2 acres on Webbs mill road, rented at $.50 per year for 15 years and then at $2.25 for balance of 99 years)	45 1/2, 70
18 May 1813	Elizabeth Campbell (W. side of Catawba R. & Sugar Cr, part of Alexander Campbell's estate; rented at $7.00 per year for 99 years)	699
18 May 1813	William Little, Sr. (on Tools Fork of Fishing Cr., W. side of Catawba R.)	236
18 May 1813	John Gordon (at juncture of Catawba R. & Sugar Cr., Story's Spring Br. & Rocky Br., Lancaster Dist.,)	172
18 May 1813	Josina Garrison (on Dutchmans Cr, W. side of Catawba R., York Dist.; rented at $2.00 per year for 99 years)	212
18 May 1813	Richard Parham (W. side of Catawba R., York Dist.; "a farm" rented at $3.90 per year for 99 years)	
18 May 1813	William Schooley (W. side of Catawba R., York Dist.; rented at $3.00 per year for 99 years)	209
31 May 1813	John Massey & George Massey (E. side of Sugar Cr., Lancaster Dist.)	84
1 Jun 1813	Thomas Hunter (Lancaster Dist.)	142
1 Jun 1813	Daniel Mills (E. side of McAlpine Cr., Lancaster Dist.; formerly Abraham Miller's; rented at $.66 per year for 99 years)	115
1 Jun 1813	John Mills (E. side of McAlpine Cr., Lancaster Dist.; rented at $.66 per year for 99 years)	115
1 Jun 1813	John B. Barron formerly Robert M. Barron's)	845
1 Jun 1813	David Houston & Aaron Houston of Mecklenburg Co. NC with James Morrison as guardian of David Houston (both sides of Six Mile Cr., Lancaster Dist.; David Houston to have 306 acres of total, rented for $2.50 per year for 99 years)	528
1 Jun 1813	John Vandigrift (on Twelve Mile Cr., Lancaster Dist.)	191
1 Jun 1813	William Potts of Mecklenburg Co, NC (E. side of 6 Mile Cr., on Long Br., Lancaster Dist.; rented at $1.00 per year for 99 years)	60
2 Jun 1813	Henry Lee (on waters of Neelys Cr., W. side of Catawba R.; rented for $2.00 per year for 99 years)	190
2 Jun 1813	George Ross, guardian of Thomas Neel (W. side of Catawba R., York Dist.; rented for $.50 per ear for 19 years and then at $3.00 for the balance of 99 years	153
2 Jun 1813	Alexander Faries (on E. side of Catawba R.; rented for $10.00 per year for 99 years)	142
2 Jun 1813	Silas Faires (formerly Alexander Faries'l	90
7 Jun 1813	Abel Barnett (Lancaster Dist.)	200
___ Jun 1813	William Erwin (formerly Patrick Hamilton's, sold to Erwin for $292	73
29 Jul 1813	Thomas Simpson (on W. corner of the Indian boundary, York Dist.; formerly Francis Adams, Esq.'s, rented at $.50 per year for 22 years and then at $2.00 for the remaining 99 years)	126
3 Aug 1813	Gabriel Davis (on Neely's Cr., W. side of Catawba R., York Dist.)	222
5 Aug 1813	John Kenmoure & John Spencer (on Neely's Cr. with road from Yorkville to Lands Ford passing through the property, York Dist.)	617
8 Aug 1813	Elias Walston (at head of Taylor's Cr., York Dist.)	108
17 Aug 1813	Thomas Bailey (on Tool's Fork of Fishing Cr., W. side of Catawba R.; rented at $2.00 per year for 99 years)	242
18 Aug 1813	Thomas Barron (W. side of Catawba R., York Dist.; rented for $.50 per year for 20 years and then at $5.00 for balance of 99 years)	109
18 Aug 1813	Jacob Jones (W. side of Catawba R., York Dist.; rented at $2.00 per year for 99 years)	108
30 Aug 1813	William Hogge	165
10 Sep 1813	John Baxter, Jr. (on Crooked Cr., E. side of Catawba R., York Dist.; formerly John Baxter, Sr.'s)	336
19 Sep 1813	John McGill (on Sugar Cr., Lancaster Dist.)	141
21 Sep 1813	John Henderson (a resurvey)	
20 Oct 1813	Henry Lee (Neelys Cr. At crossroads of McClennahan's Road and Patton's Road, York Dist.; rented for $1.50 per year for 99 years)	161
20 Oct 1813	Thomas McClellan & Elias B. McClellan (on Watson's Br. Of Fishing Cr.)	276
20 Oct 1813	Robert Neely (on Half Mile Cr., W. side of Catawba R., York Dist.; rented for $.50 per year for 9 years then at $4.50 per year for balance of 99 years)	202
12 Nov 1813	James Johnston & James Harris (fork of Mill Cr. & Sugar Cr.; York Dist.; formerly Hugh Ticer's)	
25 Dec 1813	Andrew Giles (formerly Thomas Black's)	252
___ 1813	Alexander Scott (E. side of Catawba R., York Dist.)	168

Date	Description	Acres
_____ 1813	John Barnes (on Tools Fork, W. side of Catawba R., York Dist.)	192 1/2
1 Feb 1814	Andrew Leathem & John Smith (W. side of Catawba R., York Dist.)	75
18 Feb 1814	James Harris (on waters of Big Sugar Cr.,E. side of Catawba R., York Dist.; formerly John Smith of Mecklenburg's; paid $150 for lease)	_____
4 May 1814	Robert Barnett (original lease on E. side of Steel Cr.,York Dist.)	162
31 May 1814	John Mills (Lancaster Dist.; transferred to George Massey same day)	84
31 May 1814	George Massey (Lancaster Dist.; formerly John Mills' of York Dist.; rented at $1.25 per year for 99 years)	84
1 Jun 1814	John Robertson (both sides of Big Allison Cr., York Dist.; rented for $2.00 per year for balance of 99 years)	202
1 Jun 1814	Thomas Davis (Neelys Cr., W. side of Catawba R., York Dist.; formerly Gabriel Davis,' rented at $3.00 per year for 99 years)	222
1 Jun 1814	Joseph Young (on Four Mile Cr.,W. side of Catawba R., York Dist.; rented at $4.00 per year for 99 years)	144
8 Jun 1814	Sarah Erwin, widow of William Erwin, Sr. (E. side of Catawba R., York Dist.; will provided that the lease granted William Erwin, Sr. be left to his widow and at her death to go to son William Erwin, Jr.)	_____
8 Jun 1814	Edmund Weathers and William Weathers, heirs of Isaac Weathers (E. side of Catawba Rd., York Dist.)	353
14 Jun 1814	Jeremiah Alderson (at mouth of Little Sugar Cr., York Dist.; site of an early Catawba Indian village, rented at $5.00 per year for 99 years)	213
14 Jun 1814	James Webb, deceased (on Blackberry Br., E. side of Catawba R., York Dist.)	1,009
14 Jun 1814	Archibald Frew (E. side of Sugar Cr., York Dist.; formerly in James Harris' estate, rented for $.50 per year to 1824 and then at $2.50 per year for balance of 99 years)	100
15 Jun 1814	Samuel Partlow (part of Long Island in Catawba R., beginning near Allison Cr., along the Indian boundary line, York Dist., rented at $10.00 for 90 years)	200
15 Jun 1814	Joseph Eakins (formerly John B. Barron's)	845
15 Jun 1814	Joseph Eakins (W. side of Catawba R., on "Old Great Road;" a part of a grant to James Simeral, rent $1.25 yearly for 99 years)	154
24 Jun 1814	Hugh Cathcart (18 acres disputed with David Dunlap)	576
8 Aug 1814	John Mills (on waters of McAlpine Cr., Lancaster Dist., formerly Abraham Miller's)	230
10 Aug 1814	Joseph White (E; side of Catawba R., York Dist.; Zebulon Jackson released 402 of 530 acres; originally Thomas Spratt's)	402
18 Aug 1814	_____ Patterson	100
25 Aug 1814	Stephen Pettus (Lancaster Dist.; formerly John Culp's, rented for $.50 per year for 14 years and then at $5.00 per year for the balance of 99 years)	513
25 Aug 1814	John Springs III (E. side of Steel Cr,, E. side of Catawba R., York Dist. Part of a survey of Jno Campbell's for J. Darnell, formerly McKinlish' [Alexander Candlish?], rented at $2.50 per year for 99 years)	124
25 Aug 1814	William Baxter (E. side of Catawba R., York Dist.; rented at $.50 per year for 12 years and then at $3.00 per year for the balance of 99 years	132
31 Aug 1814	Alexander Houston	208
15 Sep 1814	Noble Boulden (W. side of Catawba R., York Dist.)	14
19 Oct 1814	Martha Ann McClellan & Jane McClellan (on Taylors Cr., W. side of Catawba R.; York Dist.; formerly Robert McClellan's)	132
19 Oct 1814	Benjamin Weathers (on McAlpine Cr. And road to Harrisburg , Lancaster Dist.)	152
19 Oct 1814	Elizabeth Knox, widow (Lancaster Dist.; originally leased by J. Greer)	516
19 Oct 1814	John White (W. side of Sugar Cr. & White Oak Br., York Dist.)	730
19 Oct 1814	John Workman (Tools Fork of Fishing Cr., W. side of Catawba R., York Dist.; original lease)	
31 Oct 1814	Archy Miller	75
21 Nov 1814	Daniel Mills (Lancaster Dist.; formerly John Mills' including 40 acres of tract bought from Abraham Miller)	129
12 Dec 1814	James Harris Est., Robert Smith & Phebe Harris, admin. (on fork of Mill Cr. & Sugar Cr., York Dist.; formerly James Johnston & James Harris')	
_____ 1814	James Harris (on Sugar Cr. & NC line; formerly John Smith's)	44
_____ 1814	Rev. John Rooker (received by sheriff's auction, formerly Willis Reeves')	120
_____ 1814	_____ Garrison (on Steel Creek, E. side of Catawba R., York Dist.; site of grist mill originally built by Theodorick Webb and later sold to Isaac Garrison)	
30 May 1815	Zebulon Wren (York Dist.; original lease to John Sellers)	163
1 Jun 1815	Thomas Hunter (rented at $1.00 per year for 99 years)	141
8 Jul 1815	Francis McWatters (on W. side of Sugar Cr., York Dist.; rented for $2.00 per year for 99 years)	164
16 Aug 1815	Joseph McCorkle (E. fork of Dutchmans Cr., York Dist.; original lease, rented for $4.00 per year for 99 years)	173
18 Aug 1815	John Burns (on Sugar Cr., Lancaster Dist.; original lease, rented at $1.25 per year for 99 years)	80
18 Aug 1815	John Dunlap (W. side of Catawba R., York Dist.)	374
18 Aug 1815	William Dunlap & James Dunlap (on Patton's Cr., W. side of road from Yorkville to McClenahan's Ferry, York Dist.; original lease, rented at $5.00 per year for 99 years)	427
18 Aug 1815	Mary Dunlap & Susannah Dunlap, daughters of George Dunlap (W. side of Catawba R. York Dist.; lease originally purchased by grandfather William Dunlap from Thomas Gary)	450
18 Aug 1815	Littleberry Patterson (York Dist.)	100
18 Aug 1815	William Moore & James Moore (on Half Mile Cr., W. side of Catawba R., York Dist.; rented at $5.00 per year for 99 years)	333
18 Aug 1815	Mary Sinclair (between waters of Allison Cr. & Dutchmans Cr., York Dist.; original lease, rented at $2.25 per year for 99 years)	112

Date	Name and Description	Acreage
___ Sep 1815	James S. Workman (on Stoney Cr., on W. side of Catawba R., York Dist.)	640
3 Oct 1815	Allsey Fuller (formerly Alexander Fairis')	110
20 Dec 1815	Abraham Miller (headwaters of Four Mile Cr., York Dist.; plat shows Nation Ford Rd. to Yorkville)	643
____ 1815	John Anderson (W. side of Catawba R., S. E. side of Lusks Run Br., of Fishing Cr., York Dist.)	519
____ 1815	Jesse Harris (E. bank of Sugar Cr., Lancaster Dist.; formerly Sarah Cheek's)	101
____ 1815	Joseph McCorkle (W. bank of middle fork of Dutchmans Cr., W. side of Catawba R., York Dist.	175
____ 1815	John Cauthen (on Half Mile Cr., W. side of Catawba R., York Dist. ; "where grist mill now stands")	25 1/2
10 Jan 1816	William Faires (formerly Alexander Faires')	178
25 Jan 1816	John Barron (W. side of Catawba R., York Dist.)	216
7 Mar 1816	Edmund Weathers (York Dist., E. side of Catawba, York Dist.; "subdivided from his father;" rented at $3.0 per year for 99 years)	147
19 May 1816	Samuel Faires (original lease from Catawba Indians, rented for $4.00 per year for 99 years))	190
20 Jun 1816	Jesse Sledge (on Six Mile Cr., Lancaster Dist.; part of lease formerly Robert Crockett's, "descended to J. Sledge by heirship")	520
21 Jun 1816	William Smiley Hamilton (original lease, rented for $.25 per year for the balance of 99 years)	51
21 Jun 1816	Abraham Miller	75
21 Jun 1816	Archible Miller	75
21 Jun 1816	Francis M.Nash (original lease, rented for $1.25 per year for 99 years)	100
20 Jul 1816	Alexander McKibben (on 12 Mile Cr., Lancaster Dist.)	50
15 Aug 1816	William Moore (E. side of Catawba R., York Dist.; "on the Big Hill near the Great Pond;" survey plat shows Indian village, formerly Andrew Herron's, lease sold by Herron to Moore for $3,600; originally Thomas Spratt's)	370
15 Aug 1816	Hugh White (E. side of Catawba R., York Dist.; originally Thomas Spratt, Sr's)	141
15 Aug 1816	John Springs III (E. side of Steel Cr., E. side of York Dist.; formerly Edmund Weathers')	147
16 Aug 1816	Jesse Brumfield (middle fork of Dutchmans Cr., W. side of York Dist.; rented at $5.50 per year for 99 years)	145
16 Aug 1816	William Gilmore & C. Gilmore (on Neelys Cr., W. side of Catawba R., York Dist.; original lease, rented at $.25 per year for 99 years)	98
16 Aug 1816	William McCorkle (on Wildcat Br., a fork of Fishing Cr., W. side of Catawba R., York Dist.; original lease, rented at $2.25 per year for 99 years)	290
20 Aug 1816	Edmund Jennings & Pam. Jennings (on Fishing Cr., W. side of Catawba R., York Dist.; rented at $.50 for 20 years and then at $2.50 per year for the balance of 99 years))	187
23 Aug 1816	John Springs III (on Crooked Br., E. side of Catawba R.; formerly John Baxter's)	29 1/4
23 Aug 1816	Robert Mursh (E. side of Catawba R., York Dist.; formerly William Pettus')	100
29 Aug 1816	Alsey Fuller (E. side of Catawba R., York Dist., near the India Hook shoals; formerly John Faris'; rented at $1.50 per year for 99 years)	112
29 Aug 1816	Alexander Scott (E. side of Catawba R., York Dist., replaced 1813 lease)	168
29 Aug 1816	Heirs of Andrew Spratt (E. side of Catawba R., York Dist.)	325
29 Aug 1816	Robert Bell (E. side of Catawba R.; original lease to Alexander Candlish, formerly James Stewart's, rented at $2.00 per year for 99 years)	125
29 Aug 1816	George Pettus (both sides Steel Cr. & NC line, E. side of Catawba R., York Dist.; originally Samuel Knox's, 50 acres of which was rented at $.50 per year for $10.00 per year for the balance of 99 years)	838, 761, 50
29 Aug 1816	Alexander Candlish (E. side of Catawba R., York Dist.)	125
30 Aug 1816	Hartwell Adkins (both sides of Dutchman Cr.; W. side of Catawba R., York Dist.; rented at $3.00 per year for 99 years)	168
30 Aug 1816	William Hogg (W. side of Catawba R., York Dist.; formerly John Fewell's, rented at $3.00 per year for 99 years)	136
	Elsey Weathers (York Dist.)	117
____ 1816	Robert Harris (E. side of Catawba R., York Dist.)	1,446
____ 1816	Cadwallader Jones (W. side of Catawba R.; formerly William Moore & James Moore's sold for $3260)	402
____ 1816	James Miller (on Catawba R., Lancaster Dist.; 3 separate leases, one acreage unknown)	203, 200
10 Feb 1817	Maj. Thomas Roach (on Tools Fork, W. side of Catawba R.; formerly Thomas Bailey's)	242
28 Feb 1817	Henry W. Smith	188
25 Mar 1817	Benjamin Sansing (on Half Mile Cr., W. side of Catawba R.; formerly Robert Neely's)	202
___ Mar 1817	James McKee (E. side of Catawba R.; formerly Arthur Erwin's)	362
22 May 1817	Joseph Miller (rented at $1.35 per year for 99 years)	30
24 Jul 1817	William Reeves (Half Mile Cr., W. side of Catawba R., York Dist.; survey by Andrew S. Hutchison)	235
9 Aug 1817	Drury Ashcraft (Cain Run Br. Of Fishing Cr., W. side of Catawba R., York Dist.)	119 1/2
12 Aug 1817	David Hutchison & John Quart (on Half Mile Cr., W. side of Catawba R., York Dist.)	230
13 Aug 1817	Joseph Stinson (S. side of Four Mile Cr., W. side of Catawba R., York Dist.; rented at $2.00 per year for 99 years)	185
13 Aug 1817	James Perry. (on Steel Cr. Rd. & Spratt's Rd., Lancaster Dist.; formerly John Merrit, Jr.'s)	75

Date	Description	Acres
13 Sep 1817	Cadwallader Jones (W. side of Catawba R., York Dist.)	288
3 Oct 1817	Silas Faires (E. side of Catawba R., York Dist.; formerly Alex Faires)	90
14 Oct 1817	William P. Thomasson (on Half Mile Cr., W. side of Catawba R., York Dist., formerly Benjamin Sansing's)	202
_____ 1817	James McKee (E. side of Catawba R., York Dist.; formerly Zebulon Jackson's)	175
_____ 1817	Nathaniel Harris (E. side of Catawba R., York Dist.; lease inherited from father, Nathaniel Harris, Sr.)	163
_____ 1817	Henry G. Harris (E. side of Catawba R., York Dist.; lease inherited from father, Nathaniel Harris, Sr.)	_____
13 Feb 1818	Bartlett Meacham (E. side of Catawba R., York Dist.; formerly James Jackson's)	105 1/2
_____ 1817	Elizabeth Falconer (formerly Benjamin Sansing's)	46 1/2
28 Feb 1818	Allen Jones Green (W. side of Catawba R.; formerly Obadiah Alexander & Margaret Neely's)	237 1/2
22 Mar 1818	Flint Hill Baptist Church (2 acres of land from William Pettus estate & another lease from Drewry Smith, signed by John Dinkins)	2
2 May 1818	John Kenmoure (W. side of Catawba R., York Dist., rented at $2.00 per year for 99 years)	617
18 May 1818	Stephen Pettus (E. side of Catawba R., York Dist.)	150
21 May 1818	Joel Bailes (W. side of Sugar Cr., "about a mile above Harrisburg,: E. side of Catawba R., York Dist.; originally Thomas Sansing's)	108
21 May 1818	Joseph Gillespie (Lancaster Dist.; original lease with Catawba Indians)	330
21 May 1818	Thomas Sansing (rented at $2.50 per year for 99 years)	107
21 May 1818	John Richardson (on Br. Of Six Mile Cr., York Dist.; rented at $.25 per year for 3 years then at $2.08 per year for the balance of 99 years))	200
21 May 1818	Churchwell Anderson & Fowler Williams (on Barkley's Br., 12 Mile Cr., Lancaster Dist.; rented at $3.00 per year for 99 years)	141
22 May 1818	John Barron (on 12 Mile Cr., York Dist.; rented for $5.50 per year for 99 years))	333
22 May 1818	William Garrison (W. side of Catawba R., York Dist.; rented at $.75 per year for 99 years)	45
22 May 1818	James Parham (on Half Mile Cr., W. side of Catawba R., York Dist.)	125
26 May 1818	James Parham (on fork of Pipestone Br. Of Half Mile Cr., on W. side of Catawba R., York Dist.; rented at $3.00 per year for 99 years)	175
___ Jul 1818	John N. Henry (on Wildcat Br., a fork of Fishing Cr., York Dist.; formerly William McCorkle's)	290
1 Aug 1818	Thomas Barron (on waters of Dutchmans Cr.; W. side of Catawba R., York Dist.; rented for $4.00 per year for 99 years.)	280
13 Aug 1818	Buckner Lanier (on Hobb Br & Rocky Br. Of Sugar Cr., E. side of Catawba R., York Dist.; rented at $10.00 per yer for 99 years)	332
13 Aug 1818	James Listenbee ("at Webb's mill pond, near the clay hole at the mill dam, on E. side of Steel Cr., York Dist.; formerly Henry W. Smith's, rented at $.50 per year for 16 years and then $3.50 per year for balance of 99 years)	188
13 Aug 1818	Mial Pair (Lancaster Dist.)	100
14 Aug 1818	Robert Bell (on Clapboard Tree Br., E. side of Catawba R., York Dist.; as guardian of John Betty and William Betty, minors, rented at $2.25 per year for 99 years)	170
14 Aug 1818	James Faris (part of island in Catawba R. on Indian line above Thorn's Ferry; rented at $5.00 per year for 99 years)	63
14 Aug 1818	James Garrison (originally to Arthur Garrison, rented at $4.50 per year for 99 years)	369
14 Aug 1818	Thomas S. Garrison (E. side of Catawba R., York Dist.; "on Bobets corner")	145
14 Aug 1818	William Gilmore, millwright (both sides of Saluda Rd, W. side of Catawba R., York Dist.; rented at $.12 per year for 99 years)	100
14 Aug 1818	Cadwallader Jones (on headwaters of Half Mile Cr., W. side of Catawba R, York Dist.; originally Matthew Neely's, formerly Allen Jones Green's, bought for $3,400, rented at $.50 per year for 10 years and then at $5.00 per year for the balance of 99 years)	230
14 Aug 1818	John Kenmoure (on waters of Neelys Cr., W. side of Catawba R., York Dist.; rented at $.50 for one year and then at $10.00 per year for the balance of 99 years)	143
14 Aug 1818	Joseph Steele (on Fishing Cr., W. side of Catawba R., York Dist.; rented at $1.91 per year for 99 years)	130
14 Aug 1818	Hugh Whitesides (on 4 Mile Cr., Rocky Br. & W. side of Catawba R., York Dist.; including 11 acres on south part of an island shared with James Whitesides who has 7 acres of the north section with sluice; rented at $5.00 per year for 99 years)	233 1/2
14 Aug 1818	William Turner Ingram (adjoining Indian line 7 "Granny's Road;" formerly Joseph Cathcart's, rented at $4.00 per year for 99 years)	306 3/4
25 Aug 1818	Thomas Robertson (on Six Mile Cr. & W. bank of Catawba R., York Dist.; rented at $3.00 per year for 99 years)	390
___ Aug 1818	John Harris (formerly Andrew Giles')	252
22 Dec 1818	Francis McWaters (Rocky Br & E. side of Catawba R., York Dist.)	153
_____ 1818	Dr. John Miller (on 12 Mile Cr., Lancaster Dist.)	887
7 Jan 1819	Samuel Caldwell & Charles Elms (E. side of Catawba R., York Dist.; formerly Parmenia Rodgers')	107
16 Jan 1819	William Garrison (formerly Elizabeth Falconer's)	46 1/2
9 Jan 1819	James H. Davis (W. side of Big Sugar Cr. E. side of Catawba R., York Dist.; originally Thomas Sansing's, formerly Parmenia Rodgers, Charles Elms & S. D. Caldwell's)	107
9 Mar 1819	Thomas Ashcraft	88
5 May 1819	John Polk (with mill pond & saw mill on 6 Mile Cr., W. side of Catawba R., York Dist.)	411
21 May 1819	Robert White (rented at $4.00 per year for 99 years)	337
21 May 1819	William M. Dickson (at James Steele's stillhouse seat on Mary Steele's Spring Br. On Main Fishing C., W. side of Catawba R., York Dist.; rented at $.50 per year for 10 years and then at $10.00 per year for the balance of 99 years)	244

Date	Description	Acres
21 May 1819	James Johnson (on Main York Rd., W. side of Catawba R., York Dist.; rented at $5.00 per year for 99 years)	132
21 May 1819	James Johnson (W. side of Catawba R., York Dist.; rented at $2.50 per year for 99 years)	126
21 May 1819	Jackson Neely (W. side of Catawba R., York Dist.; rented at $.50 per year for 99 years)	215
21 May 1819	Robert Robinson (on 6 Mile Cr., W. side of Catawba R., York Dist.; rented at $.25 per year for 8 years and then at $5.00 for balance of 99 years)	202
21 May 1819	John Jackson (on Spratt's Br. & Steel Cr., E. side of Catawba R., York Dist.)	515
21 May 1819	Robert Spencer (at mouth of Flat Rock Br., NW side of Taylor's Cr., W. side of Catawba R., York Dist.; an original lease, rented at $2.50 per year for 99 years)	315
24 May 1819	Robert Robinson (fomerly Robert Linn's, rented at $..25 per year for 8 years and then at $8.00 per year for the remainder of 99 years)	202
29 May 1819	Samuel Steele (on Tools Fork of Fishing Cr., W. side of Catawba R., York Dist.)	356
1 Jul 1819	John McClanahan, Sr. (W. side of Catawba R., York Dist.)	1025
4 Jul 1819	William Polk (on Ten Mile Cr., W. side of Catawba R., York Dist.; an original lease, rented at $10.00 per year for 99 years)	516
8 Jul 1819	Francis McWatters (on Rocky Br. & Fishing Cr., W. side of Catawba R., York Dist.)	164
8 Jul 1819	James Kinnear (E. side of McAlpine Cr.; Lancaster Dist.; formerly James Miller's)	102
8 Jul 1819	Alexander Houston (York Dist.; an original lease, rented at $5.00 per year for 99 years)	208
8 Jul 1819	James Kimbrel	176
8 Jul 1819	James Davis & _____ Crockett (E. side of Catawba R., York Dist.; $2.50 annual rent, formerly Henry Coltharp's)	83
8 Jul 1819	James Davis & _____ Crockett (E. side of Catawba R., York Dist.; 12 & one/half cents annual rent, formerly Henry Coltharp's)	02
8 Jul 1819	John Kimball (E. side of Catawba R., York Dist.; original lease, rented at $2.00 per year for 99 years)	137
8 Jul 1819	James Miller (E. side of McAlpine Cr. On NC line, Lancaster Dist.; formerly James West's, rented at $.50 per year for 99 years)	44
9 Jul 1819	David Webb (W. side of Catawba R., York Dist.; original lease, paid $3.50 per year for 99 years)	195
9 Jul 1819	Samuel Burns, blacksmith (on old Indian path, S. side of Four Mile Cr., W. side of Catawba R, York Dist.; rented at $8.00 per year for 99 years)	600?
29 Jul 1819	John B. Hall (original lease on Fishing Cr., W. side of Catawba R., York Dist.; rented at $2.00 per year for 99 years)	119
29 Jul 1819	John McElwain (rented at $.50 per year for 11 1/2 year and then at $5.00 per year for the balance of 99 years)	148 1/2
29 Jul 1819	Joseph Carrol (W. side of Catawba R., York Dist.; rented for 29 years at $6.33 per year for the balance of 99 years)	511
29 Jul 1819	John Carrol (W. side of Catawba R., York Dist.; rented at $.50 per yer for 29 years and then at $6.33 per year for the balance of 99 years)	524
29 Jul 1819	Minor Carroll	1058
29 Jul 1819	John McClanahan (W. side of Catawba R., York Dist.; rented at $5.00 per year for 99 years)	102
29 Jul 1819	Benjamin Morrow (both sides of Tar Kill Br. In Lancaster Dist.; rented at $.25 per year for 99 years)	103
29 Jul 1819	John Porter (N. side of 12 Mile Cr., Lancaster Dist.; rented at $2.00 per year for 99 years)	228
30 Jul 1819	Daniel Bartlett (E. side of Steel Cr.; rented at $2.50 per year for 99 years)	145
___ Jul 1819	William Goodrich (E. side of Catawba R., York Dist.; heir of Matthew Goodrich)	215
-- Jul 1819	John Goodrich (E. side of Catawba R., York Dist.; heir of Matthew Goodrich)	145
16 Aug 1819	John Vickers (on Six Mile Cr., W. side of Catawba R.; York Dist.)	221
11 Sep 1819	William Moore (on N. W. side of the Saluda Rd.; after 1830 to pay $4.00 rent yearly & the sum of 50 cents yearly until that time or the value in goods or chattels, due on 1st day of January)	951
11 Sep 1819	Cadwallader Jones (W. side of Catawba R., York Dist.; rented at $8.50 per year for 99 years)	402
11 Sep 1819	Lemuel Thomasson (rented at $2.00 per year for 99 years)	97
11 Sep 1819	John Vickers (W. side of Catawba R., York Dist.; rented at $2.00 per year for 99 years)	221
14 Sep 1819	David Morrow of Mecklenburg Co., NC (Lancaster Dist.; formerly Benjamin Morrow's)	103
23 Sep 1819	Nathan Kimbrell (E. side of Dutchmans Cr., W. side of Catawba R., York Dist.; formerly Jacob Jones')	108
23 Sep 1819	Nathan Kimbrell (on Sugar Cr. & Steel Cr., E. side of Catawba R., York Dist; formerly James Garrison & Benjamin Garrison's)	430
26 Nov 1819	John Springs III (at Stephen Webb's Mill Pond, E. side of Catawba R., York Dist.)	39
8 Oct 1819	Samuel B. Hutchison (both sides of Dutchmans Cr., W. side of Catawba R., York Dist.; original lease, rented for $3.33 per year for 99 years)	146
8 Oct 1819	Six Mile Presbyterian Church (Lancaster Dist.; formerly John Hutchison estate, Benjamin Harper for religious committee of Six Mile Church for 25 cents yearly rent)	5 1/2
8 Oct 1819	John Polk (on Six Mile cr., W. side of Catawba R., York Dist.; original lease of 99 years for $14 rent per year)	411
18 Oct 1819	John Polk (on Six Mile Cr., W. side of Catawba R., York Dist.; formerly 3 parts (16 1/2, 39 1/2 & 111 acres) of Hugh Cathcart's, rented at $.50 per year for 99 years)	167
26 Nov 1819	John Springs (E. side of Catawba R., York Dist., at Stephen Webb's mill pond)	39
23 Dec 1819	Cadwallader Jones (W. side of Catawba R., York Dist.; formerly Lemuel Thomasson's)	97
23 Dec 1819	Cadwallader Jones (W. side of Catawba R., York Dist.; formerly Samuel Henry & Jackson N. Henry's, rented for $6.00 per year for 99 years)	202
____ 1819	James Lisenbee	90 3/4
25 Feb 1820	John Jackson (formerly George Givens')	100
17 Mar 1820	John Niven (E. side of Catawba R., York Dist.; rent for 3 years $8.81 with portion to Alexander Stewart for .93 3/4 cents rent)	____

17 Mar 1820	Alexander Stewart (rented for 93 3/4 cents per year)	
17 Apr 1820	William Faires (includes mouth of India Hook; Hezekiah Thorn, Jonathan Neely & William Faires' interest combined, formerly held by Samuel Dinsmore)	169 1/2
20 Apr 1820	William Montgomery & Samuel Montgomery (S. side of Taylors Cr., W. side of Catawba R., York Dist.; part of 2 original surveys, one of 105 acres bought from David McCain & 47 acres from Thomas McCullough)	152
13 May 1820	Robert W. Carnes (on Six Mile Cr., Lancaster Dist.)	11 1/4
14 Jul 1820	Andrew Heron (rented at $2.00 per year for 99 years)	50
14 Jul 1820	Dr. William Moore (E. side of Catawba R., York Dist.; 1/2 of ferry landing)	50
14 Jul 1820	James Spratt (E. side of Catawba R., York Dist.; 1/2 of ferry landing)	50
14 Jul 1820	Elias McClellan (W. side of Catawba R., York Dist.; rented at $1.75 per year for 99 years)	120
14 Jul 1820	Samuel Montgomery (W. side of Catawba R., York Dist.; oiginal lease, rented at $4.50 per year for 99 years)	152
15 Jul 1820	Henry G. Harris (E. side of Sugar Cr., Lancaster Dist.)	157
15 Jul 1820	William Shirling (E. side of Catawba R., York Dist.)	170
21 Jul 1820	John Starr (Tools Fork of Fishing Cr., York Dist.)	208
27 Jul 1820	Dr. Charles M. Hanna (both sides of Fishing Cr., W. side of Catawba R., York Dist.)	102
5 Aug 1820	Ann Garrison (W. side of Catawba R., York Dist.; rented at $10 per year for 99 years)	516
5 Aug 1820	Ann Garrison (W. bank of Catawba R., York Dist.; taxes paid by Austin Garrison, no date)	369
5 Aug 1820	Thomas Neel (W. side of Catawba R., York Dist.; lease negotiated by James Campbell, attorney for Neel)	453
28 Sep 1820	Samuel Ticer of NC (on Four Mile Cr., W. side of Catawba R.; York Dist.)	174
30 Sep 1820	Cadwallader Jones (on Half Mile Cr., W. side of Catawba R., York Dist.; formerly Lemuel Thomasson's)	202
2 Oct 1820	Samuel Elliott (E. side of Catawba R., York Dist.; formerly Thomas S. Garrison's, $8 per acre, signed in presence of David Hutchison but no Indian commissioner's name is on the document)	145
7 Oct 1820	Jesse Spencer (both sides of Taylors Cr., W. side of Catawba R., York Dist.; a gift from his father, Thomas Spencer, rented at $.12 per year for an undetermined time and then at $1.00 per year for the balance of 99 years)	134
7 Oct 1820	Thomas Dunlap (on waters of Neelys Cr., W. side of Catawba R., York Dist.; formerly John Kenmour's)	52
21 Nov 1820	Samuel Hutchison (W. bank of Catawba R., York Dist.)	39
25 Nov 1820	Henry Tally (on Fishing Br. & Rocky Br., W. side of Catawba R.; York Dist.; formerly Francis McWatters')	164
_____ 1820	Joseph Hunter (Millstone Br., Lancaster Dist.; formerly Simon Climer's)	121
_____ 1820	Cadwallader Jones (W. side of Catawba R., York Dist.; formerly Mary Thomasson's)	202
_____ 1820	John Doby (Lancaster Dist.; formerly John Robertson's)	174
6 Jan 1821	Thomas Ticer (Lancaster Dist.; formerly Samuel Ticer's)	
12 Jan 1821	Robert P. Workman (on Tool's Fork of Fishing Cr., York Dist.; from estate of John Workman, Sr.)	150
12 Jan 1821	John Workman (on Tools Fork of Fishing Cr., W. side of Catawba R., York Dist.; from estate of John Workman, Sr.)	150
13 Jan 1821	Alexander Moore (formerly J. E. Jennings')	187
25 Jan 1821	William W. Pettus (in India Hook Hills, E. side of Catawba R., York Dist.; formerly Jesse Farris')	479
26 Jan 1821	John Springs III (E. side of Catawba R., York Dist.; formerly George Pettus')	888
29 Jan 1821	Bartlett Meacham (E. side of Steel Cr., E. side of Catawba R., York Dist.	297
29 Jan 1821	James McKee (E. side of Catawba R., York Dist.; 340 acres formerly Arthur Irwin's; 284 acres formerly Robert Harris'; 373 acres formerly Zebulon Jackson's; 159 acres formerly Merrit & Crow's)	1056
30 Jan 1821	James Graham (formerly John Merrit's, originally Robert Simpson's)	109
20 Feb 1821	Willis Pierce (W. side of Catawba R., York Dist.; formerly William Hogge's)	136
21 Feb 1821	Samuel Roach (formerly Noble Boulden's)	14
24 Mar 1821	William Barron (W. side of Catawba R., York Dist.; formerly Joseph Eakin's)	845
-- Mar 1821	John Springs (formerly Spell Kimbrell's)	200
25 Apr 1821	Flint Hill graveyard (formerly Alexander Scott's & sold to Benjamin Person for Flint Hill Baptist Ch.)	
14 Aug 1821	Robert Fee (rented at $.50 per year for 99 years)	126
16 Aug 1821	John Steele (rented at $1.50 per year for 99 years)	138
6 Sep 1821	James Miller (mouth of Cheraw Br., E. side of Sugar Cr., Lancaster Dist.; rened at $2.00 per year for 99 years)	214
7 Sep 1821	Samuel Hutchison (original lease)	315
7 Sep 1821	Joseph M. Strain (on Garrison's Br., Dutchman's Cr., W. side of Catawba, York Dist.; rented at $1.32 per year for 99 years)	91
12 Sep 1821	School House Spring to John Soward (formerly held by Ann Garrison, admx of David Garrison's estate, to be used for benefit of the school during the term of the written lease)	
24 Sep 1821	Alsey Fuller (E. side of Catawba R., York Dist.; formerly Silas Faires')	66

Date	Description	Acres
3 Oct 1821	Cadwallader Jones (on Half Mile Cr. Near the old ford, W. side of Catawba R., York Dist.; formerly James McMeen & Elizabeth McNair's)	123 1/4
5 Oct 1821	Cadwallader Jones (W. side of Catawba R., York Dist.; formerly William Neely's)	44
5 Oct 1821	Cadwallader Jones (on Indigo Br., W. side of Catawba R., York Dist.; formerly James Thomasson's)	125
13 Oct 1821	Elias Robertson (N. side Dutchmans Cr., W. side of Catawba R.; 369 of the acres were formerly held by Benjamin Garrison	427
30 Nov 1821	John Coltharp (W. side of Big Sugar Cr., E. side of Catawba R., York Dist.; inherited from father, Henry Coltharp)	83
28 Dec 1821	David Parks (formerly Hillkeah Tally's)	——
_____ 1821	Caddwallader Jones (W. side of Catawba R., York Dist.; formerly James Thomasson's)	125
_____ 1821	Peter Acock (E. side of Catawba R., York Dist.; paid (in full) $74.35 to William Pettus estate)	——
_____ 1821	John Collier (E. side of Catawba R., York Dist.; rented land from William Pettus estate)	——
_____ 1821	David Merrit (E. side of Catawba R., York Dist.; rented land from William Pettus estate)	——
3 Jan 1822	Wylie Jones (between waters of Allison Cr. & Dutchmans Cr., W. side of Catawba R., York Dist.; formerly Robert Sinclair's)	112
7 Feb 1822	Capt. John Hutchison (Horse-Hunting Rd. & Turkey Hill, White Oak Br., "Kings Bottoms," E. side of Catawba R., Lancaster Dist.; paid $800 bounty)	520?
6 Mar 1822	John Springs III (E. side of Catawba R., York Dist.; formerly William Thomasson's)	——
27 Apr 1822	Sterling Russell (W. side of Big Sugar Cr., E. side of Catawba R., York Dist.; formerly John Coltharp's)	83
6 Jun 1822	John Hart & Elie Bigger (W. side of Catawba R., York Dist.; rented at $1.75 per year for 99 years)	109
6 Jun 1822	Samuel B. Pettus (rented at $.50 per year for 4 1/2 years and then $2.50 per yer for the balance of 99 years)	150
6 Jun 1822	Robert Bell (W. side of Steel Creek, E. side of Catawba R., York Dist.; a "side lease" of George Pettus' inherited by John DOK Pettus)	150
6 Jun 1822	John Springs (rented in two parrcels at rates of $3.75 and $3.00 per year for 99 years)	300
6 Jun 1822	John Springs (E. side of Steel Cr., E. side of Catawba R., York Dist.; rented at $2.00 per year for 99 years)	247
6 Jun 1822	John Springs (W. side of Steel Cr., E. side of Catawba R., York Dist.; mill dam and mill pond; originally leased to Nathaniel Irwin	330
6 Jun 1822	Stephen Pettus (W. side of Steel Cr., E. side of Catawba R., York Dist.; formerly Robert Bell's)	150
7 Jun 1822	Jacob Jones (formerly Thomas Douglas', rented at $1.40 per year for 99 years)	100
18 Jul 1822	John Springs (E. side of Catawba R., York Dist.; 3 Indian leases & 2 deedsof land from William Pettus estate, Samuel K. Pettus, agent)	——
7 Nov 1822	Sterling Russell (W. side of Sugar Cr., E. side of Catawba R., York Dist.; sold the lease back to John Coltharp from whom he purchased the lease on 27 April 1822)	83
30 Nov 1822	James Ross (on Neelys Cr.,W. side of Catawba R., York Dist.; formerly Henry Lee's)	161
_____ 1822	David J. Rice & Eliza A. Rice (W.side of Catawba R., York Dist.; son and widow of David B. Rice received 2/9th part of estate)	444
_____ 1822	Daniel Sturgis (W. bank of Catawba R., York Dist.; formerly Drewry Wilson's)	94
20 Feb 1823	John Culp (formerly Stephen Pettus')	513
___ Feb 1823	William Thomasson (on Wildcat Cr., a fork of Fishing Cr. Waters, W. side of Catawba R., on the Saluda Rd., York Dist.;	290
14 Mar 1823	Benjamin Person (E. side of Catawba R., York Dist.)	105
28 Jul 1823	William Gilmore (W. side of Catawba R., York Dist.; paid $450 to "Thos Neel of State of Georgia, Hancock Co.")	453
1 Aug 1823	Richard Spears (Lancaster Dist.; formerly Walter Davis')	132
12 Aug 1823	John Hart (N. side of Dutchmans Cr., W. side of Catawba R., York Dist.)	427
30 Aug 1823	William Dunlap (both sides of Ten Mile Cr., on road to McClenahan's Ferry, W. side of Catawba R., York Dist.)	146
30 Aug 1823	John Dunlap (both sides of Ten Mile Cr., N. side of road to McClenahan's Ferry, W. side of Catawba R., York Dist.)	516
26 Sep 1823	Robert Douglas (W. side of Plum Br., York Dist.; formerly widow of Robert McClellan, Priscilla McClellan's)	78
1 Nov 1823	Richard Spears (Lancaster Dist.; formerly William Spears'; originally James Spears')	70
7 Nov 1823	William Sturgis (mill on W. side of Catawba R.; former lessors: David Wilson, John Hart & Daniel Sturgis, Randolph Mitchel, William Baxter, Zebulon Wrenn's; William Sturgis paid $150 to Wrenn)	7
12 Dec 1823	Dr. Buckner Lanier (Lancaster Dist.; "from the lands of James Morrow")	204
9 Jan 1824	Benjamin Garrison (survey on river bend of Catawba R. & 10 acres on the lower end of an island in the Catawba R.)	179
14 Jan 1824	David Webb (on Fishing Cr., W. side of Catawba R., York Dist.; formerly John B. Hall's)	119
15 Jan 1824	Dr. J. H. Clawson (W. side of Catawba R., York Dist.; formerly heirs of Robert McClellan's)	132
24 Feb 1824	Robert Fee (W. side of Catawba R., York Dist.; formerly John B. Hall's)	119
5 Mar 1824	Willis Hogge (on Four Mile Cr. & Six Mile Cr., W. side of Catawba R., York Dist.)	250
12 Apr 1824	Jane McQuilliams (formerly Joseph Laney's)	110
22 Apr 1824	John Chambers (on Fishing Cr., W. side of Catawba R.)	451
13 May 1824	Andrew Spratt (E. side of Catawba R.; Lancaster Dist.)	100
13 May 1824	Robert Harris (E. side of Catawba R., York Dist.; rented at $24.75 per year for 99 years)	1,446
13 May 1824	Dr. Buckner Lanier (between Catawba R. & Camden Rd., Lancaster Dist.;formerly Francis McWatters, rented for $2.00 a year for 99 years)	153

Date	Description	Acres
13 May 1824	Dr. Buckner Lanier (rented at $3.77 per year for 99 years)	203
13 May 1824	John Parks Moore (on Rocky Br. & road to bridge over Big Sugar Cr., Lancaster Dist.; rented at $2.40 per year for 99 years)	322
13 May 1824	Mary Guire alias Wilkinson (on McAlpine Cr., Lancaster Dist.)	70
13 May 1824	John K. Crockett (both sides of Six Mile Cr., Lancaster Dist.)	305
13 May 1824	James Clark of Camden (at confluence of Sugar Cr. & McAlpine Cr., plat shows millpond on Sugar Cr.& bridges over Sugar Cr. & McAlpine Cr..)	255
13 May 1824	Agnes Cathcart, widow (at head of Wildcat Cr., W. side of Catawba R., York Dist.)	269
13 May 1824	David Hagins (on Hobs Br. Of Sugar Cr., Lancaster Dist., formerly Andrew Spratt's, rented at $.50 per year and then $3.77 for balance of 99 years)	150
13 May 1824	Robert W. Carnes (on Millstone Br., Lancaster Dist.; formerly Andrew Spratt's, rented at $1.68 per year for 99 years)	211
13 May 1824	Robert W. Carnes (Lancaster Dist.; rented at $.42 per year for 99 years)	11
13 May 1824	Thomas Reason Miles (Sugar Cr. Waters of Lancaster Dist.)	153
13 May 1824	Thomas Reason Miles (on Cheraw Br., E. side of Sugar Cr., Lancaster Dist.; rented at $.25 per year for 99 years)	50
14 May 1824	William Barrow (rented at $3.25 per year for 99 years)	210
14 May 1824	Samuel Hutchison (rented at $11.00 per year for 99 years)	39
14 May 1824	William Hagens (rented at $10.00 per year for 99 years)	212
14 May 1824	James Harper (on Morrison's Cr., York Dist.; surveyed 8 Jan 1814, rented at $.50 per year for 99 years)	125
14 May 1824	John Massey (in bend of Catawba R.'s, Lancaster Dist.; formerly Henry Massey's, originally Col. William Hagins')	212
5 Jul 1824	James McKee (E. side of Catawba R., York Dist.; rented at $14.60 per year for 99 years)	1, 065
15 Jul 1824	Wilson Allen (on Tar Kill Br. & Long Br., Lancaster Dist.; formerly Andrew Spratt's, rented at $4.00 per year for 99 years)	242
15 Jul 1824	Andrew Spratt (on Tar Kill br., Lancaster Dist.; formerly Wilson Allen's)	297
15 Jul 1824	James McKee (E. bank of Catawba R., York Dist.)	1,056
15 Jul 1824	George Williams (on both sides of Six Mile Cr., Lancaster Dist.)	538
15 Jul 1824	Isaac Rosser (Lancaster Dist.)	108
16 Jul 1824	Gray Morgan (on Six Mile Cr., Lancaster Dist.)	235
16 Jul 1824	Josina Garrison (W. side of Catawba R.; York Dist.; rented at $1.50 per year for 99 years)	106
16 Jul 1824	William Love (on waters of Neelys Cr., W. side of Catawba R.; formerly Joseph Daniels')	110 3/4
16 Jul 1824	Willis Hogge (rented at $3.25 per year for 99 years)	242
16 Jul 1824	Joseph Miller (rented at $4.83 per year for 99 years)	330
16 Jul 1824	Jackson Spenser (on bank of Taylors Cr., W. side of Catawba R., York Dist.; rented at $.10 per year for 10 years and $3.00 for balance of 99 years)	234
17 Jul 1824	Robert Douglas (rented at $1.25 per year for 99 years)	78
6 Aug 1824	Betsy Ears or Ayres , Catawba Indian (Kings Bottoms, on Catawba R., Lancaster Dist.; formerly Catawba Queen Sally New River's)	534
29 Oct 1824	John M. Doby (Kings Bottoms on Catawba R., Lancaster Dist.; formerly Catawba Indians Lewis Canty & Sally Ayres;)	502
29 Oct 1824	Robert Tilghman (on Spratt's Br. & Poplar Spring Br.; formerly Daniel Smith's, originally Samuel Knox's heir, William Pettus)	113
29 Oct 1824	John D. Smith (W. side of Steel Cr., E. side of Catawba R.; formerly Daniel Smith's)	401
29 Oct 1824	John Springs III (W. side of Steel Cr. & W. side of Tuckaseegee Rd; formerly Stephen Pettus,' originally leased by his grandfather, Samuel Knox, rented at $1.50 per year for 99 years)	223
30 Dec 1824	John Starr (formerly Maj. Thomas Roach's)	208
_____1824	Elias Garrison (on middle fork of Dutchmans Cr., W. side of Catawba R., York Dist.)	115
_____1824	Robert Stinson (original lease, rented for 99 years)	191
_____1824	James M. Harris (on Johnny's Town Br., E. side of Catawba R., York Dist.; formerly Robert Harris')	113
7 Apr 1825	Samuel Campbell (E. side of Catawba R., York Dist.; formerly John Springs')	223
12 Feb 1825	William Faires (paid $30 to Jesse Faires for lease)	10
12 Feb 1825	Jesse Faires (E. side of Catawba R.; formerly Alsey Fuller's)	20 1/4
10 Mar 1825	Thomas Patton & William Wylie (on Six Mile Cr., York Dist; rented at $.50 per year for 99 years)	206
26 Mar 1825	Samuel Chambers (purchased at sheriff's sale, formerly Jane McQuilliams')	110
7 Apr 1825	Samuel Campbell (E. side of Catawba R., York Dist.; formerly John Springs', originally Samuel Knox's)	223
6 May 1825	John Springs III (E. side of Steel Cr., York Dist.; part of original lease granted to Benedict Alderson & part to Nathaniel Erwin; rented at $.10 per year for 11 years and then at $1.00 per year for the balance of 99 years)	327
1 Jun 1825	James Miller (rented at $1.00 per year for 99 years)	
3 Jun 1825	William Carrothers (near India Hook shoals, W. side of Catawba R, York Dist.; rent of $3.33 per year to being in 1828)	200, 81 1/4
4 Jun 1825	Harvey J. Cathcart (rented at $4.00 per year for 99 years)	78

Date	Name	Acres
21 Jul 1825	Hugh Harris	208
5 Aug 1825	Littleton Bennett (rented at $3.25 per year for 99 years)	223
5 Aug 1825	James L. Bennett	221
5 Aug 1825	William Potts (Lancaster Dist.; rented at $1.00 per year for 99 years)	101
5 Aug 1825	Joseph Mitchell (rented at $.25 per year for 99 years)	44
5 Aug 1825	John Cauthen (on Half Mile Cr., "where a grist mill now stands on the bank of the Cr. Near a stone quarry," W. side of Catawba R., York Dist.; rented at $.85 per year for 99 years)	25 1/2
5 Aug 1825	Daniel Sturges (on Fishing Cr., W. side of Catawba R., York Dist.; rented at $1.06 per year for 99 years)	86
6 Aug 1825	James Buchanan (on bank of Tools Fork, W. side of Catawba R., York Dist.; rented at $.87 per year for 99 years)	112
6 Aug 1825	Silas Buchanan (W. side of Catawba R., York Dist.; rented at $.87 per year for 99 years)	50
6 Aug 1825	William Montgomery (on Tinkers Cr., a branch of Fishing Cr.; formerly James Kenmoure's, annual rent of $1.00 for 99 years)	105
6 Aug 1825	Thomas Spencer, Jr. (on Half Mile Cr. & S. side of Yorkville Rd., W. side of Catawba R., York Dist.; rented at $50 per year for 9 1/2 years and then at $1.50 per year for the balance of 99 years)	109
6 Aug 1825	John M. Doby (Kings Bottoms on Catawba R., Lancaster Dist.; original lease formerly Betsey Ayres or Betsy Ears, Catawba Indian, rented at $10.00 per year for 99 years)	534
6 Aug 1825	Elizabeth Roddey, widow of David Roddey (on Harris' Rd & Neelys Cr., W. side of Catawba R., York Dist.; rented at $5.00 per year for 99 years)	348
6 Aug 1825	Thomas Simpson (York Dist.; rented at $1.50 per year for 99 years)	102
7 Aug 1825	John Hutchison on Kings Bottoms, Catawba R., Lancaster Dist.; formerly John M. Doby's)	502
7 Aug 1825	Robert Robinson (both sides of Steel Cr. Rd., rented at $.62 per year for 99 years)	100
12 Aug 1825	John Burns (Lancaster Dist.)	80
14 Aug 1825	James McKee (W. side of Sugar Cr., E. side of Catawba R., York Dist.)	——
15 Aug 1825	Joseph Mitchell (on Dutchman's Cr., W. side of Catawba R., York Dist.; formerly Lewis Talbert's)	44 1/2
2 Sep 1825	Spell Kimbrell (W. side of Steel Cr. above where it empties into Sugar Cr.)	105
2 Sep 1825	Stephen Pettus (E. side of Catawba R., York Dist.; rented at $.75 per year for 99 years)	150
2 Sep 1825	John Springs III (W. side of Steel Cr., E. side of Catawba R., York Dist.; formerly Stephen Pettus')	117
2 Sep 1825	John Steel (on Plum Br., W. side of Catawba R., York Dist.; rented at $2.50 per year for 99 years)	199
2 Sep 1825	Stephen Pettus (E. side of Catawba R. York Dist.; formerly Jesse Farris')	150
2 Sep 1825	Stephen Pettus (W. side of Steel Cr., on Doby's Rd., E. side of Catawba R, York Dist.; bought from William Campbell, admr. Of Samuel Campbell)	117
14 Sep 1825	John P. Moore (E. side of Sugar Cr., Lancaster Dist.)	61
4 Oct 1825	James Miller (E. side of Catawba R., Lancaster Dist.; formerly William Crockett's)	155
21 Oct 1825	Robert Bell, Guardian for John Betty & William J. Betty (on Clapboard Br., E. side of Catawba R., York Dist.; "formerly William Betty's, one of the legatees of John Betty, by Matthew Goss, attorney")	170
3 Nov 1825	Jerome Miller (W. side of Catawba R., York Dist.; formerly Dr. J. H. Clawson's)	132
22 Nov 1825	Richard J. Miller (on Hob Br. & Long Br., E. side of Sugar Cr., Lancaster Dist.; formerly David Hagins')	63
2 Dec 1825	Stephen Pettus (at bridge on E. side of Steel Cr., E. side of Catawba R., York Dist.; formerly George Pettus, Sr.'s)	150
_____ 1825	James Miller (on McAlpine Cr., Lancaster Dist.; formerly James West's)	42
_____ 1825	Drury Morrow (on Hob Br. & Long Br., E. side of Sugar Cr., Lancaster Dist.; formerly Richard J. Miller's)	63
28 Feb 1826	John Springs (formerly Richard Springs; sold for $551)	100
4 Mar 1826	Robert Watson ("lying on main road leading from Charlotte, N. C. to Doby's Bridge, S. C.," Lancaster Dist.; formerly Seymour Taylor's)	176
6 Mar 1826	Francis Spencer (on Half Mile Cr., W. side of Catawba R., York Dist.; formerly Thomas Spencer's)	109
31 Mar 1826	Edmund Jennings (W. side of Catawba R., York Dist.; formerly James Mason's)	——
5 Jun 1826	Andrew Spratt (Lancaster Dist.; formerly John Thompson's, bought at sheriff's sale for $140)	100
8 Jun 1826	James Miller (on both sides of road from Yorkville to Lands Ford, W. side of Catawba R., York Dist.; inherited from Jesse Miller)	188
15 Jun 1826	William Potts of Mecklenburg, NC (on "old trading road" in Lancaster Dist.; rented at $.62 and 1/2 cents per year for 99 years)	208
16 Jun 1826	Frederick Ezzell (on 12 Mile Cr. And mill road, Lancaster Dist.; rented at $.37 per year for 99 years)	112
16 Jun 1826	Benjamin Morrow (on Sugar Cr., Lancaster Dist.; rented at $6.25 per year for 99 years)	270
17 Jun 1826	Rachel McCullough & 4 daughters Dorothy McCullough, Mary McCullough, Sarah McCullough & Rachel McCullough (on Fishing Cr., W.side of Catawba R., York Dist.; formerly John Anderson's)	73 1/2
21 Jul 1826	John Hagins (on Morrison Cr., W. side of Catawba R., York Dist.; rented at $.50 per year for 12 years then at $10.00 per year for the balance of 99 years)	309
21 Jul 1826	John Moore (Lancaster Dist.; rented for 99 years)	82 1/2
21 Jul 1826	Hugh Harris (on Rocky Br., "at the old Ford;" original lease to Samuel W. Ruddock, rented at $.50 per year for 99 years)	139
21 Jul 1826	Thomas Robertson (on Taylors Cr., a branch of Fishing Cr., W. side of Catawba R., York Dist.; rented at $5.00 per year for 99 years)	273
21 Jul 1826	Anson Sizer (on Six Mile Cr. & Sugar Cr., Lancaster Dist.)	162

Date	Description	Acres
24 July 1826	John Starr (W. side of Catawba R., York Dist.; rented at $2.00 per year for 99 years)	208
25 Jul 1826	Holoway E. Simmons (originally surveyed for Nancy George, Catawba Indian; rented at $2.00 per year for 99 years)	80
29 Aug 1826	Robert Bell (E. side of Catawba R., York Dist.)	125
4 Oc t 1826	Thomas Faris (between waters of Allison Cr. & Dutchmans Cr., W. side of Catawba R., York Dist.; formerly Wylie Jones')	112
13 Oct 1826	Alfred R. Hutchison (formerly Samuel Hutchison's; attested by Cynthia Hutchison)	315
23 Oct 1826	David Hyatt	19 1/2
16 Nov 1826	Dr. H. J. Cathcart (W. side of Catawba R., York Dist.)	81 1/5
16 Nov 1826	William Cathcart (W. side of Catawba R., York Dist.)	34 1/5
25 Nov 1826	James McKee (W. side of Steel Cr., E. side of Catawba R., York Dist.; formerly John D. Smith's)	401
18 Dec 1826	William Lawson (Lancaster Dist.; formerly John Robinson & Dr. Buckner Lanier's who acquired the lease from David Morrow)	103
1 Jan 1827	Thomas Allen (on E. side of Cain Br. Of Fishing Cr., W. side of Catawba R., York Dist.; formerly Robert McClelland's)	567
1 Jan 1827	John Springs III (E. side of Catawba R., York Dist.; formerly Robert Bell's)	125
4 Jan 1827	James Lessley (on Neely's Cr., W. side of Catawba R., York Dist.; formerly James Ross')	161
25 Jan 1827	James Barron, Robert M. Barron (on Dutchman's Cr., W. side of Catawba R.; inherited 3/4ths of Thomas Barron, Sr.'s lease)	462
25 Jan 1827	Archibald Barron (on Dutchmans Cr., W. side of Catawba R., York Dist.; inherited 1/4th of Thomas Barron, Sr.'s lease)	154
20 Jan 1827	Jesse Faires (W. side of Johnny's Town Br., E. side of Catawba R., York Dist.; formerly Brownlee Harris and Robert Harris')	1446
24 Feb 1827	H. J. Cathcart (on Dutchman's Cr., W. side of Catawba R., York Dist.; formerly Samuel Chambers')	110
3 Mar 1827	James Johnson (on Tools Fork, W. side of Catawba R., York Dist.; formerly Silas Buchanan's)	50
5 Apr 1827	James P. Henderson (originally John Henderson's)	
14 Apr 1827	Capt. John Moore (E. side of Sugar Cr., Lancaster Dist.)	150
14 Apr 1827	James Ross (on Sugar Cr., Lancaster Dist.; formerly Leroy Springs')	150
20 Mar 1827	Josander Garrison (on Barkley's Br. of Fishing Cr., W. side of Catawba R., York Dist.formerly Josina Garrison's)	377
5Jun 1827	Robert W. Gill (Lancaster Dist.; bought at sheriff's sale, "Perry & McKensie vs. Thos. R. Miles")	100
12 Jul 1827	William Cathcart (W. side of Catawba R.)	34 1/2
24 Jul 1827	William Carrothers (W. side of Catawba R., York Dist.; rented at $.87 per year for 99 years)	81
27 Jul 1827	Stanhope Sadler (on Tools Fork of waters of Fishing Cr., W. side of Catawba R., York Dist.; originally leased to William McMurray)	182
27 Jul 1827	Benjamin Chambers of Yorkville (W. side of Catawba R., York Dist.; rented at $.30 per year for 13 years and then at $4.00 per year for the balance of 99 years)	497
27 Jul 1827	John Evans (on "Old Indian Trading Road" and Four Mile & Six Mile Cr.'s, W. side of Catawba R., York Dist.; rented at $10.00 per year for 99 years)	734, 132
27 Jul 1827	William Ardrey (formerly William Miller's)	102
27 Jul 1827	William B. Henderson (near Saluda Rd., W. side of Catawba R., York Dist.; rented at $5.00 per year for 99 years)	220
27 Jul 1827	John Thompson (W. side of Catawba R., York Dist.; rented at $10.00 per year for 99 years)	204
27 Jul 1827	Robert McClelan (on Taylors Cr, W. side of Catawba R., York Dist.; resident of Lancaster Dist.; rented for $5.00 per year for 99 years)	345
27 Jul 1827	Charles M. Hanna (rented at $2.00 per year for 99 years)	102
27 Jul 1827	Stanhope Sadler (on Tools Forks, W. side of Catawba R., York Dist.; formerly James Johnston's, originally leased to William McMurray; rented for $2.50 per year for 99 years)	474
27 Jul 1827	Samuel Campbell (W. side of Steel Cr., E. side of Catawba R., York Dist.; original lease rented at $1.25 per year for 99 years)	150
27 Jul 1827	Samuel Campbell (W. side of Steel Cr., E. side of Catawba R., York Dist.)	223
27 Jul 1827	John Cauthen (formerly William Baxter's, rented at $3.00 per year for 99 years)	132
28 Jul 1827	Daniel Shaw (on Dutchmans Cr., W. side of Catawba R., York Dist.)	75 1/2
5 Aug 1827	Holoway E. Simmons (W. side of Catawba R., York Dist.; rented at $5.00 per year for 99 years)	277
10 Aug 1827	David Hagins (E. side of Sugar Cr. & Long Br., Lancaster Dist.; formerly James Ross')	150
14 Aug 1827	Gray Westbrook (on Lusks Run of Fishing Cr., W. side of Catawba R., York Dist.; rented for $2.50 per year for 99 years)	186
21 Aug 1827	Alfred R. Alexander (W. side of Catawba R., York Dist.; rented at $3.50 per year for 99 years)	184
21 Aug 1827	Holoway E. Simmons (on Neely's Cr., E. side of Columbia Rd., W. side of Catawba R., York Dist.; bought at sheriff's sale, formerly John McElmoyle's, rented for $.50 per year for 99 years)	165
25 Aug 1827	David Patton (on W. bank of Catawba R, York Dist.; rented at $6.00 per year for 99 years)	408
25 Aug 1827	James Ross (on Long Br., Lancaster Dist.; rented at $3.10 per year for 99 years)	150
25 Aug 1827	William Miller (formerly Thomas Neel's)	365
1 Sep 1827	William Amberson (E. side of Catawba R., York Dist.)	497
10 Oct 1827	David Hagins (on Hob Br. of Six Mile Cr., Lancaster Dist.; formerly James Ross')	150
11 Oct 1827	Dr. William Moore (E. side of Catawba R., York Dist.; 3 leases including 1/2 of ferry, 50 acres; Indian village shown on plat)	370, 276

Date	Description	Acres
20 Nov 1827	Robert Saville (E. side of Catawba R., York Dist.; formerly Nathaniel Harris, ' sold at a sheriff's sale)	150
20 Dec 1827	Herbert Lanier (mouth of Fishing Br. & Rocky Br., near Doby's Bridge, E. side of Catawba R., York Dist.; formerly Henry Tally's)	164
26 Dec 1827	Joshua Gordon (E. side of Six Mile Cr., "below Daniel Morrow's old saw mill," Lancaster Dist.; a sublease for 15 years from George Williams with a small piece of land to be enclosed at $3 an acre)	———
____ 1827	Robert Harris (E. side of Catawba R., York Dist.; formerly Alsey Fuller's)	20 1/4
____ 1827	Samuel Chambers (both sides of Dutchmans Cr., W. side of Catawba R., York Dist.; formerly Hartwell Adkins'	168
____ 1827	James Perry (E. side of Catawba R., York Dist.; purchased from Stephen Webb for $1925)	225
1 Jan 1828	John Henderson, John Wright, Dr. ____ Miller (on S. prong of Dutchmans Cr., W. side of Catawba R., York Dist.; formerly Nathaniel Thomasson's)	133 1/3
2 Jan 1828	Thomas Whitesides (Lancaster Dist.,; formerly Robert Gill's)	———
3 Jan 1828	James Spratt (E. side of Catawba R., York Dist.)	230
5 Feb 1828	Thomas Faries (W. side of Catawba R., York Dist.; fomerly Wiley Jones')	112
10 Mar 1828	John Springs III (on Nation Ford Rd., E. side of Catawba R., York Dist.; formerly William Goodrich')	45 3/4
27 Apr 1828	Hugh Harris (near Thorn's Ferry on Catawba R., York Dist.)	121 1/2
7 Jul 1828	William Mason (E. side of Catawba R., on Steel Creek)	200
18 Jul 1828	John Springs Roach (W. side of Wildcat Cr., W. side of Catawba R., York Dist.; from his brother Thomas Roach, Jr., who inherited the lease from their father, Thomas Roach, Sr.)	50
5 Aug 1828	H. E. Simmons (W. side of Catawba R., York Dist.)	165
6 Aug 1828	Robert Fee of Chester Dist. (on Tinkers Cr., a Br. of Fishing Cr., W. side of Catawba R.; original lease from Head Men of Catawba Indians)	126
4 Sep 1828	Gilbert Shaw (N. side of Dutchmans Cr., W. side of Catawba R., York Dist.; rented at $1.00 per year for 99 years)	77
4 Sep 1828	William Thorn	196
5 Sep 1828	William Carrothers (W. side of Catawba R., York Dist.; rented at $1.50 per year for 99 years)	183
5 Sep 1828	Nancy McCaw (on Little Allison Cr., W. side of Catawba R., York Dist.; 693 acres rented for $8.00 per year for 99 years)	693, 592
5 Sep 1828	Joseph Michael (W. side of Catawba R., York Dist.; rented at $.50 per year for 99 years)	33
5 Sep 1828	William Thorn (York Dist.; rented at $1.00 per year for 99 years)	173
5 Sep 1828	Robert Stearn (rented at $1.25 per year for 99 years)	110
5 Sep 1828	Andrew Shillinglaw (on Four Mile Cr., W. side of Catawba R., York Dist.; rented at $1.00 per year for 99 years)	74 1/2
19 Sep 1828	James Carrothers (W. side of Catawba R., York Dist.; rented at $3.33 per year for 99 years)	234
19 Sep 1828	John R. Patton (on N. fork of Neely's Cr., W. side of Catawba R., York Dist.; formerly Elizabeth Patton's)	154
19 Sep 1828	John O'Neal (W. side of N. fork of Neelys Cr., W. side of Catawba R., York Dist.; rented at $2.81 per year for 99 years)	144
___ Sep 1828	Nancy McCaw	330
20 Nov 1828	John P. Moore (on Allison Cr., near Hill's Old Iron Works, W side of Catawba R., York Dist.; formerly John Robinson's with small section to John Patton)	174
20 Nov 1828	John Robinson (E. side of Sugar Cr., Lancaster Dist.; formerly David Hagins and James Ross')	150
24 Dec 1828	Joseph Douglass (on waters of Allison Cr. & Dutchmans Cr., W. side of Catawba R., York Dist.; formerly Wylie Jones & Thomas Farriss')	116
____ 1828	George P. White, Hugh M. White, Joseph F. White (E. side of Catawba R., York Dist.; three sons of Hugh White to have equal shares of river bottom land and upland by his will)	908
6 Jan 1829	Matthew Miller (formerly John Springs III')	200
14 Jan 1829	Leroy Secrest (Lancaster Dist.; formerly Buckner Lanier's)	203 1/2
7 Jan 1829	John Springs (E. side of Catawba R., York Dist.; formerly William Withers')	65
29 Jan 1829	James Davis (E. side of Catawba R., Lancaster Dist. , on McAlpine Cr.; same sold by John Coltharp on Oct. 23, 1829 to Joel Bailes)	107
13 Feb 1829	James Miller (formerly James West's)	44
20 Feb 1829	Henry G. Massey (Lancaster Dist.; formerly William Hagins')	212
9 Mar 1829	Wylie Pitman (on Columbia Rd & Neelys Cr., W. side of Catawba R., York Dist.)	50 1/2
6 Apr 1829	Reuben House (on Sugar Cr., E. side of Catawba R., York Dist.; formerly Dr. Buckner Lanier's at suit of A. H. Herron)	400
30 May 1829	Francis M. Nash (W. side of Catawba R., York Dist.; formerly A. H. Herron's, rented at $1.50 per year for 99 years)	203
30 May 1829	Joseph Hunter (on Millstone Br., E. side of Sugar Cr., Lancaster Dist.)	129
25 Jul 1829	Henry Fewell (York Dist.)	112
22 Aug 1829	Major Temple Hall (on Dutchmans Cr., W. side of Catawba R., York Dist.; formerly Joseph Mitchell's)	44 1/2
14 Nov 1829	Leroy Secrest (on Hobs Br., E. side of Catawba R., Lancaster Dist.; formerly David Hagins')	150
20 Nov 1829	John Robinson (E. side of Sugar Cr., Lancaster Dist.; formerly James Ross & David Hagins')	150
21 Nov 1829	John Lawson Kendrick (on Dutchmans Cr., W. side of Catawba R., York Dist.; formerly M. T. Hall's)	44 1/2
29 Dec 1829	Joseph F. White (E. side of Catawba R., York Dist.; formerly Zebulon Jackson's)	402
30 Jul 1829	Joseph Hunter (Lancaster Dist.; rented at $1.00 per year for 99 years)	121

8 Jan 1830	James Davis (formerly John Springs III's)	125
11 Jan 1830	John Bell (formerly James Davis')	125
14 Feb 1830	David Parks (on waters of Johnny's Town Br., E. side of Catawba R., York Dist.)	20
5 Mar 1830	Allen Morrow (Lancaster Dist.; paid $3 per acre)	97
8 May 1830	William Potts of Mecklenburg Co., NC (Lancaster Dist.; rented at $49 per year for 99 years)	50
8 May 1830	Joseph Hagins (W. side of Catawba R., York Dist.; rented at $.50 per year for 99 years)	36
8 May 1830	Joseph Hagins (on Morrison Cr.; W. side of Catawba R., York Dist.; rented at $2.00 per acre for 99 years)	122
8 May 1830	John M. Doby (on 12 Mile Cr., near the mouth of Kings Br.; Lancaster Dist.; rented at $3.00 per year for 99 years)	200
16 Jul 1830	Bealy Sizer (Lancaster Dist.; rented at $2.82 per year for 99 years)	435
16 Jul 1830	David Hagins (Lancaster Dist.; rented at $2.68 per year for 99 years)	417
16 Jul 1830	James Johnson (Fewell's Fork of Fishing Cr., W. side of Catawba R., York Dist.; formerly J. H. I. Cathcart's)	203
16 Jul 1830	John Polk (W. side of Catawba R., York Dist.)	39 1/2
16 Jul 1830	John Polk (on Six Mile Cr., York Dist.; rented for 50 bushels of corn per year for 99 years)	324
6 Aug 1830	John Roddey (on Neely's Cr., W. side of Catawba R., York Dist.; formerly held by his mother, Elizabeth McTeer Roddey, widow, original lease to David Roddey)	202
12 Aug 1830	Robert Collier (on the E. side of Catawba R., York Dist.; rented at $1.30 per year beginning in 1837)	187
13 Aug 1830	William B. McCain (on the Lincoln Rd., W. side of Catawba R., York Dist.; rented at $2.00 per year for 99 years)	180
13 Aug 1830	James Reeves (W. side of Catawba R., York Dist.; rented at $4.44 per year for 99 years)	143
20 Aug 1830	John Scott (on 10 Mile Cr. & 6 Mile Cr., W. side of Catawba R., York Dist.; rented at $.50 per year for 99 years)	263
21 Aug 1830	Harvey J. Cathcart (W. side of Catawba R., York Dist.; rened at $1.25 per year for 99 years)	83
21 Aug 1830	Philip Sandefur (W. side of Catawba R., York Dist.; sold to Bennett Adkins sometime later in 1830; rented at $1.00 per year for 99 years)	119
21 Aug 1830	William S. May (on waters of Fishing Cr., W. side of Catawba R., York Dist.; rented at $.50 per year for 99 years)	54
21 Aug 1830	Benjamin Person (E. side of Catawba R., York Dist.; rented at $.25 per year to 1835)	199 1/2
21 Aug 1830	Benjamin Person (E. side of Catawba R., York Dist.)	105
21 Aug 1830	Alexander Strain	182
22 Aug 1830	Flint Hill Baptist Church (E. side of Catawba R., York Dist.; liberty to use the spring, arranged by Benjamin Person)	2 1/2
27 Aug 1830	William Richardson	168
27 Aug 1830	Alexander Fewell (W. side of Catawba R., York Dist.)	498
30 Aug 1830	James Perry (W. side of Catawba R., York Dist.)	297
12 Sep 1830	William Thorn & Gilbert Shaw (N. side of Dutchmans Cr., W. side of Catawba R., York Dist.)	15 7/8
2 Oct 1830	John T. Hagins (on W. bank of Catawba R., York Dist.)	148
2 Oct 1830	Benjamin Person (E. side of Catawba R., York Dist.)	200
2 Oct 1830	John Roddey (W. side of Catawba R., York Dist.; "there being no other heirs of Elizabeth Roddey except John and David Roddey, they are the proper heirs," rented at $2.94 per year for 99 years)	202
6 Oct 1830	James Lynn (on Four Mile Cr. & Six Mile Cr., W. side of Catawba R., York Dist.; formerly Willis Hogg's, bought for $600)	250
10 Oct 1830	George Ross & Francis Miller, trustees of Mary Sutton & children (W. side of Sugar Cr., E. side of Catawba R., York Dist.)	200
20 Oct 1830	John Roddey (on waters of Neelys Cr., W. side of Catawba R., York Dist.)	230
25 Oct 1830	Benjamin Garrison (E. side of Catawba R., York Dist.; rented at $7.75 per year for 99 years)	189
25 Oct 1830	Eli Bigger (formerly Samuel Reeves)	96
27 Oct 1830	Joseph Miller, Sr. (formerly Thomas Simpson's)	126
17 Nov 1830	Joseph McCorkle (formerly James Baxter's estate)	353 1/2
18 Nov 1830	Stephen Pettus (E. side of Catawba R., York Dist.: formerly held by William Campbell, admin. of Samuel Campbell's estate)	223
___ Nov 1830	John Bell (W. side of Steel Cr., York Dist.; formerly James Davis,'originally Alexander Candlish's)	125
8 Dec 1830	Thomas Patton (Neely's Cr., York Dist.; formerly James H. Whitesides & James F. Lesley's)	190
_____ 1830	Archibald Hammell (on Dutchmans Cr., W. side of Catawba R., York Dist.; formerly John Forbis,' rented at $2.50 per year for 99 years)	100
_____ 1830	James Hagins (E. side of Sugar Cr., York Dist.; formerly John P. Moore's)	174
_____ 1830	John Springs III (W. side of Steel Cr., York Dist.; formerly Robert Bell's, originally Alexander Candlish's)	125
_____ 1830	James Davis (W. side of Steel Cr., York Dist.; formerly John Springs,'originally Alexander Candlish's)	125
_____ 1830	George Steele (Middle Dutchman's Cr., York Dist.; rented at $5.00 per yer for 99 years)	209
_____ 1830	John Massey (on Morrisons Cr., York Dist; formerly James Harper's)	125

Date	Name and Description	Acres
1830	Alexander Fewell (on Dutchman's Cr. W. side of Catawba R., York Dist.)	151 1/2
1830	William E. White (W. side of Catawba R., York Dist.; formerly William Ticer's)	____
1830	Thomas McCullough (on Lusks Run of Fishing Cr., W. side of Catawba R., York Dist.; formerly John Anderson's)	150
1830	Robert Anderson (on Lusks Run of Fishing Cr., W. side of Catawba R., York Dist.; formerly John Anderson's)	150
2 Apr 1831	Rebecca Jones (Lancaster Dist.; formerly William Potts of Mecklenburg's)	101, 50
13 May 1831	John Cauthen (on Half Mile Cr., W. side of Catawba R., York Dist.; rented at $8.89 per year for 99 years)	364
20 May 1831	Jacob Clawson (W. side of Catawba R., York Dist.; rented at $1.50 per year for 99 years)	103
20 May 1831	Thomas F. Dunlap (W. side of Catawba R., York Dist.; rented at $.50 per year for 99 years)	100
20 May 1831	William B. Dunlap (on Ten Mile Cr., York Dist.; rented at $3.50 per year for 99 years)	786
20 May 1831	John Polk (W. side of Catawba R., York Dist.)	324
20 May 1831	Elizabeth Polk (W. side of Catawba R., York Dist.; formerly John Polk's who leased the land to David Dunlap & Dunlap sold the same to William Polk, deceased husband of Elizabeth, rented at $2.50 per year for 99 years)	111
16 Jul 1831	Mary Ellis (rented at $3.33 per year for 99 years)	100
16 Jul 1831	Aquilla Dyson (on waters of Fishing Cr., W. side of Catawba R., York Dist.; formerly Andrew McConnell's)	62
12 Aug 1831	Samuel H. Smith of Lancaster Dist. (on Neelys Cr., Br. of Fishing Cr., W. side of Catawba R, York Dist.; paid Ezekiel Hall $1,000 for lease)	414
13 Aug 1831	James Perry (rented at $4.33 per year for 99 years)	297
13 Aug 1831	Alexander T. Stewart (on Sugar Cr., E. side of Catawba R., York Dist.; rented at $6.66 per year for 99 years)	432
21 Aug 1831	Flint Hill Baptist Church (formerly Benjamin Persons' with proviso "at liberty to use water from spring")	2 1/2
6 Sep 1831	Charles S. Cline (W. side of Catawba R., York Dist.; formerly Thomas Dunlap's)	100
6 Oct 1831	Cadwallader Jones (W. side of Catawba R., York Dist.; formerly Dr. Jacob H. Clawson's)	103 1/2
12 Oct 1831	Samuel Smith of Lancaster Dist. (on Neelys Cr., W. side of Catawba R., York Dist.; formerly Ezekiel Hall's)	414
25 Oct 1831	John Fewell (W. side of Catawba R., York Dist.; formerly Dr. Charles M. Hanna's)	102
11 Nov 1831	Thomas Patton (W. side of Catawba R., York Dist.; formerly Robert Fee of Chester Dist.'s)	126
22 Nov 1831	D. D. Hunter (on Fishing Cr., W. side of Catawba R., York Dist.)	134
5 Dec 1831	R. S. Bedon (on 6 Mile Cr., W. side of Catawba R., York Dist.; formerly John Polk's)	411
6 Dec 1831	James Perry of Lancaster Dist. (formerly J. P. Hunter's & sold in a sheriff's sale & immediately wold to Henry Hunter for $15.00)	100
16 Dec 1831	Walter Izard (W. side of Catawba R., York Dist.; formerly William B. Dunlap's)	213 1/2
1831	William E. White & Chambers (on Poplar Spring Br., E. side of Catawba R., York Dist.: formerly William Candlish's, originally Samuel Knox's)	113
3 Jan 1832	John Craig (W. side of Catawba R., York Dist.; formerly Alexander Houston & John Polk's)	208
26 Jan 1832	Benjamin Story (at Still House Br. of Neelys Cr., W. side of Catawba R., York Dist.; formerly Thomas Patton's)	126
-- Jan 1832	Allen Richardson (on Br. of 6 Mile Cr., W. side of Catawba R., York Dist.; formerly John Richardson's)	200
2 Feb 1832	James Johnston, Phillip Sandifur & Minor Sadler (W. side of Catawba R., York Dist.; formerly estate of James F. Wallace)	35
9 Feb 1832	Eli Moore (on Neelys Br. of Fishing Cr., W. side of Catawba R., York Dist.; formerly part of Daniel Davis' lease)	60
24 Feb 1832	James L. Wright (on Mill Cr., a branch of Catawba R., York Dist.; paid Col. William Wright $662 for the tract)	158
8 Mar 1832	James Smith Miller (E. side of Sugar Cr., Lancaster Dist.; formerly McQuinney Ward's, bought for $650, had grist and sawmill)	____
14 Mar 1832	John Miller Doby (Lancaster Dist.; formerly Robert Robinson's)	100
24 Apr 1832	Drury Morrow (on Sugar Cr., Lancaster Dist.; formerly John Burns')	80
28 Apr 1832	William Sturgis (W. side of Catawba R., York Dist.; formerly James Darnell's)	177
4 May 1832	William B. Dunlap (W. side of Catawba R., York Dist.; survey of 44 acres inherited from father, plus 44 acres inherited by his brother, James Dunlap)	88
4 May 1832	William B. Dunlap (at juncture of Lands Ford Rd. & Old Pinckney Rd, near Patton's Cr., W. side of Catawba R., York Dist.)	309
29 May 1832	Peter K. Kee (W. side of Catawba R., York Dist.; rented at $5.84 per year for 99 years)	190
19 Jul 1832	Henry Caton (on Tools fork, W. side of Catawba R., York Dist.; formerly David McIlwain's, rented at $.25 per year for 99 years)	49 1/4
20 Jul 1832	John Robinson (on confluence of Sugar Cr. & McAlpine Cr., including the village of Harrisburg, Lancaster Dist.; formerly Dan C. Clark's)	255
20 Jul 1832	James Dunlap (on Landsford Rd at juncture of Old Pinckney Rd., W. side of Catawba R., York Dist.; rented at $2.50 per year for 99 years))	309
20 Jul 1832	William Faris, Sr. (on Wild Cat Br., W. side of Catawba R., York Dist.)	112
20 Jul 1832	Andrew McConnell (rented at $1.25 per year for 99 years, "a farm")	____
20 Jul 1832	Dan C. Clark (York Dist.; rented at $3.50 per year for 99 years)	255
20 Jul 1832	Sam Robinson (rented at $1.00 per year for 99 years)	150
20 Jul 1832	Philip Sandifer (on Tool's Fork of Fishing Cr., W. side of Catawba R., York Dist.; formerly James F. Wallace's, rented at $1.04 per year for 99 years)	71

Date	Description	Acres
24 Jul 1832	John Rosser (Lancaster Dist.; formerly Leroy Secrest's)	203 1/2
25 Jul 1832	James Hagins (Hobs Br. of Sugar Cr., Lancaster Dist.; formerly Leroy Secrest's)	150
31 Jul 1832	James M. Hagins (fomerly James Ross's)	174
13 Aug 1832	Minor Sadler (on Tools Fork of Fishing Cr. & McElwain's Spring Br., N. bank of Charles McElwain's Spring Br. to mouth of Rocky Cr., W. side of Catawba R., York Dist.; rented at $1.80 per year for 99 years)	131
20 Aug 1832	Charles McElwain (on Tools Fork of Fishing Cr., W. side of Catawba R., York Dist.; formerly William McMurray's, originally Isaac Smith's "old corner." Rented at $60 per year for 99 years)	44
26 Aug 1832	Hugh H. Carothers (on Dutchmans Cr., W. side of Catawba R., York Dist.; formerly John L. Kindrick's)	44 1/2
31 Aug 1832	Miss Susan Spratt (on Harrisburg Rd., E. side of Catawba R., York Dist.; survey by Benj. F. Withers on this date)	135
4 Sep 1832	William B. Dunlap (on 10 Mile Cr., W. side of Catawba R., York Dist.)	44
15 Sep 1832	Meadow White (W. side of Catawba R., York Dist.)	119 1/2
18 Sep 1832	James Whiteside & Robert Whiteside (W. side of Catawba R., York Dist.; formerly Solomon Simpson's)	189
19 Oct 1832	David Hutchison (W. side of Catawba R., York Dist.; formerly James Reeves'. sold for $600)	143
19 Nov 1832	John McCain (W. side of Catawba R., York Dist.; formerly Willis Pierce's)	136
30 Nov 1832	Eli Hartness (on waters of Johnny's Town Br., E. side of Catawba R., York Dist.; rented at $1.33 per year for 99 years)	70
19 Dec 1832	John Steele (on Saluda Rd., W. side of Catawba R., York Dist.; formerly Jeremiah Cureton's)	100
____ 1832	Alexander Strain (rebted at $2.22 per year for 99 years)	123
____ 1832	William E. White (W. side of Catawba R. including the Nation Ford Crossing; a large grist mill was built at the site in partnership with John Springs III)	816
6 Mar 1833	William McKenna of Lancaster Dist. (on Sugar Cr., W. side of Catawba R., York Dist.; formerly Alexander T. Stewart's)	432
__ Mar 1833	Edward Smith (E. side of Catawba R., on N. C. line, York Dist.; formerly Samuel Knox Pettus')	225
9 May 1833	William E. White (on Steel Cr. Rd., E. side of Catawba R., York Dist.; formerly Daniel Niven's)	____
25 May 1833	John J. Blair (; formerly Dan C. Clark's)	255
28 Aug 1833	William Potts & John Fincher (on Tar Kill Br. of Six Mile Cr., Lancaster Dist.; formerly heir of James Morrow & Susannah Morrow's)	____
30 Aug 1833	James Miller (both sides of road from Yorkville to Landsford on waters of Half Mile Cr., W. side of Catawba R., York Dist.; formerly Jesse Miller's, rented at $3.50 per year for 13 years and then at $3.50 per year for balance of 99 years)	188
31 Aug 1833	John Baxter (on Horseshoe Br., S. of Nation Ford crossing, E. side of Catawba R., York Dist.	150
8 Sep 1833	John Sitgreaves (W. side of Catawba R., York Dist.; rented at $10.00 per year for 99 years)	1,312
11 Sep 1833	Leroy Secrest (Hobs Br., Lancaster Dist.; formerly James M. Hagins')	188
18 Sep 1833	George D. Beckham (on Hobs Br., Lancaster Dist.; "as security for endorsing note in Bank" for Leroy Secrest for $600)	150
28 Sep 1833	George W. Doby (on Old Town Br., Lancaster Dist.; rented at $5.20 per year for 99 years)	550
28 Sep 1833	George W. Doby (Lancaster Dist.)	280
28 Sep 1833	Adam Ivy (on S. side of Old Town Br. & Catawba R., Lancaster Dist; original lease, rented at $3.00 per year for 99 years),	759
12 Oct 1833	Wylie Reeves (W. side of Catawba R., York Dist.; sold to him by David Hutchison for $700)	143
15 Oct 1833	Joel A. Mitchell (E. side of Catawba R., York Dist.; formerly Ivy Tilghman's, inherited from his father, Joshua Tilghman)	200
16 Nov 1833	Andrew Spratt (Lancaster Dist.; formerly Thomas Whitesides')	____
28 Nov 1833	Drury Morrow (on Millsone Br., Lancaster Dist.; formerly Robert W. Carnes')	211 1/2
23 Dec 1833	Alexander Fewell (W. side of Catawba R., York Dist.; from father, John Fewell, the tract called Wright Place)	315
23 Dec 1833	Joseph McCorkle (W. side of Catawba R., York Dist.; fomerly Alexander Fewell's)	112
____ 1833	John Tilghman (E. side of White's Cr., E. side of Catawba R., York Dist.; heir of Joshua Tilghman, had "good grist mill on it")	100
____ 1833	Ivy Tilghman (E. side of White's Cr., E. side of Catawba R., York Dist.; heir of Joshua Tilghman)	250
1 Jan 1834	John Massey (Lancaster Dist.; formerly Henry G. Massey's)	212
23 Jan 1834	Joshua Perry Smith (E. side of Catawba R., York Dist.; formerly a sublease of Bartlett Meacham, Ex'or of John Jackson, dec'd)	____
23 Jan 1834	George Pettus, Jr. (, W. side of Steele Creek, E. side of Catawba R.; formerly James Powell's)	100
4 Feb 1834	James McElwee (on the crossroads near the blacksmith shop of James L. Wright, on Mill Cr., a branch of the Catawba R., York Dist.; paid William Wright $662 for the tract)	150
24 Feb 1834	Stanley Fewell (W. side of Catawba R., York Dist.; formerly Alexander Moore's)	187
24 Feb 1834	Cadwallader Jones (W. side of Catawba R., York Dist.; site of a grist mill and stone quarry, formerly John Cauthen's)	26
7 Mar 1834	James Sadler (on Fishing Cr., W. side of Catawba R., York Dist.; formerly Richard Sadler's)	127
8 Mar 1834	Henry Caton (W. side of Catawba R., York Dist.; formerly James Johnson's who bought it from Silas Buchanan	11 1/2
10 Mar 1834	Isaac Rosser & David Hagins (on Tar Kill Br. of 6 Mile Cr., Lancaster Dist.; formerly William Potts & John Fincher's)	____
27 Mar 1834	John McElwayne (rented for 99 years)	114
2 Apr 1834	Dan C. Clark (E. side of Steel Cr.; taken from James Listenbee by suit)	189

19 Apr 1834	Matthew McCants & John McCants (formerly Samuel McWhood's)	241
4 Aug 1834	Thomas Simpson (W. side of Catawba R., York Dist.; formerly Philip Sandefur's)	119
20 Aug 1834	Joseph Hagins (both sides of 6 Mile Cr., Lancaster Dist.; formerly Samuel Robinson's)	150
24 Sep 1834	James Meacham (E. side of Catawba R., York Dist.; formerly Benjamin Persons')	
3 Oct 1834	Benjamin Ellis (W. side of Catawba R., York Dist.)	206
4 Oct 1834	Joseph Crook & James M. Crook (formerly William Ingram's)	306 3/4
17 Oct 1834	George Duren Beckham (E. side of Sugar Cr., Lancaster Dist.; original lease, rented at $1.24 per year for 99 years)	207
17 Oct 1834	Jesse Sledge (on 12 Mile Cr., Lancaster Dist.)	150
31 Oct 1834	William Neely & William Sturgis (W. side of Catawba R., York Dist.; formerly John Hart's)	275
13 Nov 1834	Wilson Allen (on 12 Mile Cr., Lancaster Dist.; formerly Jesse Sledge's)	150
7 ___ 1834	Allen Morrow (at junction of 6 Mile & 12 Mile Crs, Lancaster Dist.; formerly Jesse Sledge's; rented at $6.21 per year for 99 years)	721
9 Jan 1835	William Barron (W. side of Catawba R., York Dist.; formerly William S. May's)	54
14 Jan 1835	Isaac A. Garrison & William D. Garrison (middle fork of Dutchmans Cr., W. side of Catawba R., York Dist.; formerly Elias Garrison's)	125
3 Feb 1835	R. B. Walker (W. side of Catawba R., York Dist.; formerly John McCain's)	136
6 Feb 1835	John Robinson of Charleston (formerly John J. Blair's, received in form of note for $879.51)	255
12 Mar 1835	W. H. Mason (on waters of Tinkers Cr., W. side of Catawba R., York Dist.; originally leased by James Kenmoure and bequeathed to his dau., Eleanor Bigham, wife of Robert Bigham)	65
27 Mar 1835	Joseph Bennett (land on Catawba R., Lancaster Dist.; rented at $.62 per year for 99 years)	124
27 Mar 1835	Joseph Bennett (Lancaster Dist.)	46
27 Mar 1835	John McElwayne (formerly estate of William Ardrey)	114
27 Mar 1835	John L. Miller (near George Sturgis' spring; W. side of Catawba R., York Dist.;)	936
29 May 1835	Eli Kimbrell (W. side of Sugar Cr. & Steel Cr., E. side of Catawba R., York Dist.; rented at $5.00 per year for 99 years)	155
29 May 1835	Solomon Kimbrell (both sides of Doby Bridge Rd., E. side of Catawba R., York Dist.; $2.50 yearly rent)	415
25 Jul 1835	Alexander Barry (W. side of Catawba R., York Dist.; rented at $1.25 per year for 99 years)	86
25 Jul 1835	John H. Barry (W. side of Catawba R., York Dist.; rented at $3.75 per year for 99 years)	355
25 Jul 1835	John H. Barry (W. side of Catawba R., York Dist.; rented at $.25 per year for 99 years)	567
25 Jul 1835	John H. Barry (W. side of Catawba R., York Dist.)	86
25 Jul 1835	Eli Bigger (W. side of Catawba R., York Dist.; rented at $4.50 per year for 99 years)	427
25 Jul 1835	William Carrothers (W. side of Catawba R., York Dist.; part of Thomas Drennan's old survey, rented at $1.25 for 99 years)	172 1/2
25 Jul 1835	Jacob Clawson (W. side of Catawba R., York Dist.; rented at $10.00 per year for 99 years)	229
25 Jul 1835	Archibald Hamill (W. side of Catawba R., York Dist.; formerly William Carrothers,' rented at $2.00 per year for 99 years))	101 3/4
25 Jul 1835	Joseph McCorkle (W. side of Catawba R., York Dist.; formerly John Fewell's, rented at $2.25 per year for 99 years)	353 1/2
22 Aug 1835	W. D. Russell (E. side of Catawba R., York Dist.; formerly John Baxter's)	150
26 Sep 1835	William Amberson (on Watson's Br. of Fishing Cr., W. side of Catawba R., York Dist.; rented at $2.00 per year for 99 years))	142 1/2
26 Sep 1835	Elizabeth R. Campbell(remted at $1.00 per year for 99 years)	96
26 Sep 1835	Matthew McCommon (on Neelys Cr., W. side of Catawba R., York Dist.; rented at $.50 per year for 99 years)	151
28 Sep 1835	John S. Sitgreaves (on 6 Mile Cr., York Dist.; formerly John Polk's)	39 1/2
15 Oct 1835	William Thomasson (formerly Alexander Strain's)	123
21 Oct 1835	Robert Collier (on Clapboard Tree Br., E. side of Catawba R.; formerly heirs of William Betty's)	170
28 Oct 1835	L. H. Massey & Thomas C. Massey (on Old Town Br., Lancaster Dist.; formerly George W. Doby's)	550
20 Nov 1835	Adam Ivy, John Mills, John Robinson, James Hagins & John Fincher, trustees of Mount Ararat Methodist Episcopal Church (on waters of 6 Mile Cr., Lancaster Dist.; formerly David Hagins & Eliza Hagins')	7 1/2
20 Nov 1835	H. J. Cathcart (W. side of Catawba R., York Dist.; formerly R. B. Walker's)	136
20 Nov 1835	Curtis Winget (Lancaster Dist.; formerly James M. Hagins')	174
21 Nov 1835	William Barron (W. side of Catawba R., York Dist.; formerly Samuel N. Hutchison & James P. Hutchison's)	146
25 Nov 1835	Henry Clark (formerly Matthew McCants & John McCants')	241
26 Nov 1835	William Newell (Lancaster Dist.; fomerly Curtis Wingate's)	174
5 Dec 1835	Daniel Shaw (rented at $1.00 per year for 99 years)	75
15 Dec 1835	Jesse Farris (E. side of Catawba R., York Dist.; formerly Wm. W. Pettus')	479
30 Dec 1835	David Roddey (Middle fork of Neelys Cr., York Dist.; formerly heirs of Robert White, John M. Doby, gdn)	337
_____ 1835	John A. Wherry (W. side of Catawba R., York Dist.; formerly William Love's, sold by constable for $21)	110 3/4

Date	Description	Acres
4 Jan 1836	W. G. Cathcart (on Dutchmans Cr., W. side of Catawba R., York Dist.; formerly James Starain's)	140
9 Jan 1836	Josinah Garrison (W. side of Catawba R., York Dist.; paid $1150 in cash for lease to Wm. B. McCain of Troupe Co., Ga.)	180 1/5
9 Jan 1836	Joseph Hagins (formerly William Thomasson's)	123
20 Jan 1836	John M. Hog___	22
3 Feb 1836	George Pettus, Jr. (E. side of Catawba R., York Dist.; formerly Mary Pettus', sold by her son Thomas N. Pettus for $183.76)	67
4 Feb 1836	Isaac Rosser (on Tar Kill Br., Lancaster Dist.; formerly Dr. Buckner Lanier's)	203 1/2
4 Feb 1836	Isaac Rosser (on Tar Kill Br., Lancaster Dist.; formerly James Morrow's)	375
24 Feb 1836	Jeremiah Alderson & James Alderson (E. side of Catawba R., York Dist.)	
15 Apr 1836	James Knox (W. side of steel Cr., E. side of Catawba R., York Dist.; formerly John Bell's)	125
24 May 1836	Bartlett Meacham (on W. side Old Nation Ford Rd., E. side of Catawba R., York Dist.; formerly Henry Meacham's)	30
2 Jun 1836	George L. McKee (E. side of Steel Cr., E. side of Catawba R., York Dist.; held formerly by Ann Barnett, widow of original leaseholder, Thomas Barnett)	
7 Jun 1836	James Stewart (on Catawba R., Lancaster Dist.; rented at $2.00 per year for 99 years)	436
17 Jun 1836	John Rosser of Kershaw Dist., SC & David Hagins (on 6 Mile Cr. & Tar Kill Br., Lancaster Dist.; rented for $5.00 per year for 99 years)	578
17 Jun 1836	Drury Morrow (on Sugar Cr., Lancaster Dist.; rented at $2.50 per year for 99 years)	206
17 Jun 1836	Jesse P. Winget (on Long Br., Lancaster Dist.; rented at $1.50 per year for 99 years)	147
20 Aug 1836	Elizabeth Douglas (rented at $2.00 per year for 99 years)	176
27 Aug 1836	James Black (on Watsons Br. of Fishing Cr., W. side of Catawba R., York Dist.; rented at $1.67 per year for 99 years)	153
27 Aug 1836	Nathaniel Thomasson (on Dutchmans Cr., W. side of Catawba R., York Dist.)	81 3/4
27 Aug 1836	Alexander T. Black (on Watsons Br., Fishing Cr., W. side of Catawba R., York Dist.; rented at $1.67 per year for 99 years))	150
27 Aug 1836	John Barron (W. side of Catawba R., York Dist.; rented at $1.50 per yer for 99 years)	141
27 Aug 1836	William Carrothers (W. side of Catawba R., York Dist.; rented at $1.75 per year or 99 years)	220
27 Aug 1836	Thomas Faris (on N. bank of island in Catawba R., York Dist.; rented at $3.33 per year for 99 years)	60
27 Aug 1836	James Fewell (Tools Fork Cr., W. side of Catawba R., York Dist.; rented at $1.37 per year for 99 years)	115
27 Aug 1836	James L. Johnson (Tools Fork of Fishing Cr., W. side of Catawba R., York Dist.; rented at $.25 per year for 99 years)	44
27 Aug 1836	Willis Pierce (W. side of Catawba R., York Dist.; rented at $1.31 for 99 years)	127
8 Sep 1836	William Culp (on Long Br, Lancaster Dist.; formerly Jesse P. Winget's)	147
1 Oct 1836	John Wolfe (on Long Br. of 6 Mile Cr., Lancaster Dist.; formerly John Robinson's)	150
7 Oct 1836	Joseph Martin (on 6 Mile Cr., Lancaster Dist.)	111
10 Nov 1836	James Finley (W. side of Catawba R., York Dist.; fomerly William Barron's)	54
25 Nov 1836	Samuel Hutchison (W. side of Catawba R., York Dist.; formerly William Barron's)	146
27 Nov 1836	John R. Wright (W. side of 12 Mile Cr., Lancaster Dist.; lease purchased for $1,000 from Wm. H. Dickey, admin. of Churchwell C. Anderson's estate)	654
7 Dec 1836	Joseph Martin (on 6 Mile Cr., Lancaster Dist.)	111
25 Dec 1836	John McClellan (W. side of Plum Br., York Dist.; fomerly Elias B. McClellan's who received land by sale of Robert Douglas)	78
26 Dec 1836	Moses Ezell (on Tar Kill Br. of 6 Mile Cr., Lancaster Dist.; formerly Andrew Spratt's)	297
28 Dec 1836	Robert McClimon (on Wildcat Br. of Fishing Cr., W. side of Catawba R., York Dist.; fomerly William Barron & R. M. Pressley's)	290
13 Jan 1837	John M. Doby (on Rocky Br., E. side of Big Sugar Cr., Lancaster Dist.; formerly John Parks Moore's)	322 1/4
18 Jan 1837	William P. Miller (on Half Mile Cr., W. side of Catawba R., York Dist.; forrmerly Francis Spencer's)	109
24 Jan 1837	Wyly L. Little (formerly Aquilla Dyson's)	62
11 Feb 1837	James Davis (on Sugar Cr., E. side of Catawba R., York Dist.; formerly Peter K. Kee's)	4
17 Feb 1837	John McCaw (N. side of Dutchmans Cr., beginning at Shaw's Spring, W. side of Catawba R., York Dist.; formerly Gilbert Shaw's)	77
1 Mar 1837	George Pettus (on Steel Cr., E. side of Catawba R., York Dist.)	23 3/4
2 Mar 1837	Eli Biggers (formerly Elizabeth R. Campbell's)	96
6 Mar 1837	George Pettus, Jr. (E. side of Catawba R., York Dist.; formerly Thomas N. Pettus')	74
7 Mar 1837	John McCoy (mouth of Flat Rock Br., NW side of Taylor's Cr; formerly Thomas Reid's)	
27 Mar 1837	John P. Miller (rented at $.50 per year for 99 years)	936
29 Mar 1837	Charles Morris (E. side of Catawba R., York Dist.; formerly William Ticer's)	96
31 Mar 1837	David S. Patton (on Four Mile Cr. & Six Mile Cr., W. side of Catawba Cr., York Dist.; lease purchased by Patton for $805 at public sale following a suit levied by Samuel Burns for $6,000 and costs on John Evans)	700
7 Apr 1837	John M. Doby (Lancaster Dist.; formerly William Newell's)	174
15 Apr 1837	Joshua P. Smith (on Old Bartlett Cr. Bottoms, E. side of Catawba R., York Dist.; formerly George Pettus')	23 3/4

Date	Description	Acres
15 Apr 1837	George Pettus (on Bartlett Cr. Bottom, E. side of Steel Cr., E. side of Catawba R., York Dist.; formerly Joshua P. Smith's)	75
17 Apr 1837	Curtis Winget (Lot #1, 60 x 300 ft. on Main St in village of Bel Air, Lancaster Dist.; formerly David Hagins')	____
1 Jun 1837	John Barnes (rented at $2.50 per year for 99 years)	170
14 Jul 1837	John Barnes	530
14 Jul 1837	William Carrothers (formerly Joseph Bennett's, rented at $.62 per year for 99 years)	124
18 Jul 1837	Jeffrey P. Winget (on 12 Mile Cr., Lancaster Dist.; formerly Wilson Allen's, originally Jesse Sledge's)	150
12 Aug 1837	Wilson M. Merritt (E. side of Catawba R., York Dist.; rented at $4.25 per year for 99 years)	229
12 Aug 1837	Henry Clark	276
12 Aug 1837	Robert Saville (E. side of Catawba R., York Dist.;"a farm," rented at $10.00 per year for 99 years)	____
22 Aug 1837	Thomas Wright (on Indian boundary line at Tinkers Cr., W. side of Catawba R., York Dist.; formerly William H. Mason's, original lease from Catawba Indians to John Kenmour, thence to James Kenmour who then laid it off to his son-in-law William Montgomery)	105
25 Aug 1837	Charles Gillespie & Andrew Gillespie (on Sugar Cr., Lancaster Dist.)	131
6 Sep 1837	William Culp (rented at $3.50 per year for 99 years)	182
9 Sep 1837	Daniel Tharp (on Catawba R. including island; formerly James Tharp's, rented at $6.50 per year for 99 years)	220
30 Sep 1837	Harris Kimbrell (E. side of Catawba R., York Dist.; E. side of Catawba R., York Dist.; rented at $2.00 per year for 99 years)	124
30 Sep 1837	James W. White (on Morrison Cr., E. side of Catawba R., York Dist.; rented at $.50 per year for 99 years)	117
30 Sep 1837	John M. Coffey (on 6 Mile Cr., Lancaster Dist.; rented at $1.43 per years for 99 years)	121 1/2
1 Nov 1837	Thomas A. Sales (E. side of Sugar Cr., Lancaster Dist.)	313
25 Dec 1837	Eli S. Kimbrell (W. side of Steel Cr. on Spratt's Br., E. side of Catawba R., York Dist.; formerly George Givens')	100
30 Dec 1837	John Belk (Long Br., Lancaster Dist.; formerly John Wolfe's)	150
____ 1837	Jere Alderson (E. side of Catawba R., York Dist.; formerly Bartlett Meacham's, original grant to James Jackson)	105 1/2
1837	Catawba Baptist Church (W. side of Catawba R., York Dist.)	2
5 Jan 1838	John Fincher of Mecklenburg (Lancaster Dist.; formerly William Lawson's)	103
11 Jan 1838	James Carothers (on Dutchmans Cr., W. side of Catawba R., York Dist.; formerly Thomas Y. Barron's)	75 1/2
14 Feb 1838	William Todd (on York Rd & 10 Mile Cr., W. side of Catawba R., York Dist.; formerly Elizabeth Polk's)	111
17 Feb 1838	John McCrory (formerly James D. Hamilton's)	51
22 Feb 1838	William Potts Estate (Lancaster Dist.)	219
2 Mar 1838	Joel S. Barnett (on Dutchmans Cr., W. side of Catawba R., York Dist.; formerly James Perry's, originally Joseph McCorkle's)	204
6 Mar 1838	William P. Hagins (W. side of Catawba R., York Dist.; formerly Charles S. Cline's)	100
21 Mar 1838	Stephen Pettus (W. side of Catawba R., York Dist.; $300 to Hugh Harris, formerly held by William Pettus, originally Samuel Knox's)	309
24 Mar 1838	James Alderson (E. side of Catawba R., York Dist.; formerly Jere Alderson's)	90 3/4
26 Mar 1838	William Newell (Lancaster Dist.; formerly Curtis Winget's)	174
27 Apr 1838	Archibald Graham (on E. side of Catawba R., York Dist.)	217
10 May 1838	Thomas Robertson (on Wildcat Br. of Fishing Cr., York Dist.)	154
14 May 1838	Andrew Ezell (on Tar Kill Br. of 6 Mile Cr., Lancaster Dist.; formerly Moses Ezell's)	297
28 Jul 1838	John Campbell (rented at $2.50 per year for 99 years)	119
28 Jul 1838	John Campbell	658
28 Jul 1838	Benjamin M. Porter (on 6 Mile Cr., Lancaster Dist.)	200
28 Jul 1838	Major Temple Hall (on Dutchmans Cr., York Dist.; rented at $6.59 per year for 99 years)	422
28 Jul 1838	James H. McElwain (W. side of Catawba R., York Dist.; rented at $6.43 per year for 99 years)	590
28 Jul 1838	John McElwain (on Camp Br., Sandy Spring Br., Long Br. & Cedar Br. of Taylor's Cr., W. side of Catawba R., York Dist.; rented at $6.43 per year for 99 years)	590
2 Aug 1838	William Carothers, admin. of James Perry's estate (on Dutchmans Cr., W; side of Catawba R., York Dist.; formerly B. Hutchison's, sold for $208)	52
11 Aug 1838	Edward Avery (bounded by Ebenezer Church land,W. side of Catawba R., York Dist.; rented at $10.00 per year for 99 years)	646
11 Ayg 1838	Edward Avery (W. side of Catawba R., York Dist.)	85
11 Aug 1838	Major T. Hall (W. side of Catawba R., York Dist.; rented at $4.72 per year for 99 years)	412 1/2
11 Aug 1838	Joseph H. White, Robert P. Harris & Algernon S. White (on Dutchmans Cr., W. side of Catawba R., York Dist.; formerly James M. Harris' rented for $4.33 per year for 99 years)	354
11 Aug 1838	James P. Hutchison (on Dutchmans Cr., W. side of Catawba R., York Dist., rented for $1.21 per year for 99 years)	141
11 Aug 1838	John R. Hall (W. side of Catawba R., York Dist.; rented at $2.00 per year for 99 years)	255
11 Aug 1838	Brownlee Harris (on waters of Morrisons Cr., W. side of Catawba R., York Dist.; rented at $.58 per year for 99 years)	117
5 Sep 1838	John Springs, Esq. (on Steel Cr. & its branches, E. side of Catawba R., York Dist.)	1045

Date	Description	Acres
7 Sep 1838	Andrew Powers (on Tools Fork waters of Fishing Cr., W. side of Catawba R., York Dist.; originally leased to William McMurray)	182
8 Oct 1838	Drury Morrow (Lancaster Dist.; formerly Benjamin Morrow's, originally James McKnight Morrow's)	173
13 Oct 1838	Samuel McDowell (S. fork of Neelys Cr., W. side of Catawba R., York Dist.; rented at $1.12 per year for 99 years)	155
16 Oct 1838	James M. Garrison (Lancaster Dist.; formerly Joseph Bennett's)	46
20 Oct 1828	William E. White (on Meadow Br & Spratt's Br., E. side of Catawba R., York Dist.; formerly Thomas Kendrick's)	140
31 Oct 1838	Henry G. Massey (both sides of Taylors Cr., W. side of Catawba R., York Dist.; formerly Jesse Spenser's)	134
9 Nov 1838	John T. Hagins (below Joseph Hagins' ferry; on White Oak Br., E. Lancaster Dist.; original lease, purchased for $600 from William Harris, acting chief of Catawba Indians, formerly inhabited by Judah Airs & John Airsm rented at $3.00 per year for 99 years)	388
13 Nov 1838	Stephen Pettus (on W. side of road leading to Thorn's Ferry & on NC line, E. side of Catawba R., York Dist.; formerly Stephen H. Tilghman's, including a grist mill known as Tilghman's Mill; rented at $3.00 per year for 99 years)	100
17 Nov 1838	John Sitgreaves (on 6 Mile Cr., W. side of Catawba R., York Dist.; formerly held by Hannah Linn, widow of Robert Linn)	202
18 Dec 1838	Jonathan Davis (on Tinkers Cr., W. side of Catawba R., York Dist.; formerly William H. Mason's & originally James Kenmoure's)	65
19 Dec 1838	Solomon Kimbrell (E. side of Catawba R., York Dist.; formerly held by Nancy Kimbrell, widow of Spell Kimbrell)	165
24 Dec 1838	B. F. Davison (Long Br., Lancaster Dist.; formerly John Belk's)	150
25 Dec 1838	James Partlow (both side of Big Allison Cr., W. side of Catawba R., York Dist.; formerly Charity Robertson and Thomas Robertson's)	202
___ Dec 1838	A. G. Graham (E. side of Catawba R., York Dist.; formerly held by the heirs of James Harris, dec'd)	96
_____ 1838	Lucy Barnes, widow of John Barnes (on Tools Fork, W. side of Catawba R., York Dist.)	192 1/2
_____ 1838	James Harper (on Catawba R.; formerly Oakley Henderson's)	81 1/4
11 Jan 1839	Samuel W. Ruddock (E. side of Catawba R., York Dist.; formerly Hugh Harris')	137
15 Jan 1839	J. A. Kuykendal (on Tools Fork, W. side of Catawba R., York Dist.)	182
18 Jan 1839	Estate of Dr. John L. Miller (on 6 Mile Cr., Lancaster Dist.)	219
25 Jan 1839	Andrew L. Davis (Lancaster Dist.; formerly part of estates of William Potts & George A. White)	57 1/2
28 Jan 1839	Jesse Farris (E. side of Catawba R., York Dist.; formerly Stephen Pettus')	309
14 Feb 1839	Samuel Roach (on Wildcat Cr., york Dist.; formerly John Springs Roach's; originally Thomas Roach's)	50
27 Feb 1839	Jesse Faires (on India Hook Cr., E. side of Catawba R., York Dist.; formerly Josiah Faris')	15
1 Mar 1839	George Pettus (E. side of Catawba R., York Dist.; formerly estate of Daniel Smith's)	100
2 Mar 1839	Eli Kimbrell (W. side of Steel Cr., E. side of Catawba R., York Dist.; formerly James McKee's)	401
6 Mar 1839	Eleazer Harris (York Dist.; formerly Joseph Kendrick's)	21 3/4
7 Mar 1839	Joseph Kendrick (E. side of Catawba R., York Dist.; from Rhoda Mursh, Catawba Indian and widow of Robert Mursh, Pamunkey Indian, originally Samuel Knox's)	31
7 Mar 1839	Samuel Faris (E. side of Catawba R., York Dist.; formerly Joseph Kendrick's)	31
15 Mar 1839	Daniel Smith (E. side of Catawba R., on Steel Cr.; formerly Nancy Mason's inherited from William Mason, Smith paid $150.00)	200
25 Mar 1839	William Barron (W. side of Catawba R., York Dist.)	184 1/2
1 Apr 1839	B. F. Davidson (on Sugar Cr., Lancaster Dist.; awarded in court case "Dunlap & Carnes vs. John Belk")	300
24 Apr 1839	Rev. P. E. Bishop (W. side of Catawba R., York Dist.; formerly Nathan Kimbrell's)	1/2
13 Jul 1839	Willis Pierce (on Dutchmans Cr., W. side of Catawba R., York Dist.; rented at $2.75 per year for 99 years))	186
13 Jul 1839	James P. Henderson (W. side of Catawba R.; annual rent of $4.62 1/2 for 99 years)	263 1/2
20 Jul 1839	John M. Doby (Lancaster Dist.; formerly Curtis Winget's)	97
23 Jul 1839	William Neely & William Sturgis (W. side of Catawba R., York Dist.; formerly John Heath's)	224
28 Jul 1839	John Campbell (on Neelys Cr., W. side of Catawba R., York Dist.; rented at $2.77 per year for 99 years	326
24 Aug 1839	Joshua P. Smith (W. side of Sugar Cr., E. side of Catawba R., York Dist.; formerly Eli Kimbrell's)	401
6 Sep 1839	WilliamCulp (lease from Catawba Indians)	182
6 Sep 1839	Nathan Kimball (W. side of Catawba R., York Dist.; rented at $.50 per year for 99 years)	459
6 Sep 1839	John H. Clark	123
9 Sep 1838	David Hagins (Lancaster Dist.; rented at $1.50 per year for 99 years)	314
10 Sep 1839	Frederick Ezell (on Tar Kill Br. of 6 Mile Cr.,Lancaster Dist.; formerly Andrew Ezell's)	297
16 Sep 1839	Joel Bailes (on McAlpine Cr., Lancaster Dist.; a "side lease")	4
20 Sep 1839	John Barron (W. side of Catawba R., York Dist.)	845
21 Sep 1839	George Cathey (E. side of Catawba R., York Dist.; rented at $1.62 per year for 99 years)	213
21 Sep 1839	Wylie Pitman ((rented at $.25 per year for 99 years)	50
21 Sep 1839	Nathan Kimball (on Flat Br. of Dutchmans Cr., W. side of Catawba R., York Dist.)	515

Date	Description	Acres
21 Sep 1839	James Stewart (rented at $2.25 per year for 99 years)	233
21 Sep 1839	James Stewart (rented at $6.50 per year for 99 years)	304
21 Sep 1839	Samuel Johnston (E. side of Catawba R., York Dist.; rented at $8.00 a year for 99 years)	567
30 Sep 1839	George R. Roach (W. side of Plum Br., York Dist.; formerly John McClellan's, who inherited the lease from his father, Robert McClellan)	78
11 Oct 1839	Aaron Houston (Lancaster Dist., on NC line)	283
11 Oct 1839	James W. White (W. side of Catawba R., York Dist.)	117
12 Oct 1839	John T. Hagins (may be the same as 9 Nov 1838 lease)	388
17 Oct 1839	James M. Harris (W. side of Catawba R., York Dist.; formerly Ann Garrison's as administratrix of David Garrison, deceased, a "side lease")	516 ?
23 Oct 1839	John Coltharp (W. side of Big Sugar Cr., about 1 mi. above Harrisburg, E. side of Catawba R., York Dist.; formerly Mary Elizabeth Davis', heir of James H. Davis)	108
23 Oct 1839	Joel Bailes (W. side of Big Sugar Cr., E. side of Catawba R., York Dist.; formerly John Coltharp's)	108
26 Oct 1839	Marcus A. Tuttle (lot in Bel Air Village, surveyed as Lot #3, 60 ft. on Main St. & 300 ft. back on which his house stands, Lancaster Dist.; Bel Air Village was formerly part of David Hagins' original lease from Catawba Indians)	
31 Oct 1839	Andrew Powers (on Tools Fork, W. side of Catawba R., York Dist.; formerly J. A. Kuykendal's)	182
1 Nov 1839	J. M. Cooper	176
1 Nov 1839	James Moore (on Half Mile Cr., W. side of Catawba R., York Dist.; rented at $6.40 per year for 99 years)	245
1 Nov 1839	James Moore (on Spratt's Br., E. side of Catawba R., York Dist.; rented at $5.00 per year for 99 years)	357
1 Nov 1839	Benjamin S. Massey (York Dist.; rented at $3.00 per year for 99 years)	85
1 Nov 1839	Benjamin S. Massey (on Kings Bottoms road, Lancaster Dist; rented at $.50 per year for 99 years)	200
1 Nov. 1839	Benjamin S. Massey (on 12 Mile Cr. & Catawba R., Lancaster Dist.; rented at $6.00 per year for 99 years)	536
1 Nov 1839	Benjamin S. Massey (on Camden-Salisbury Rd., Lancaster Dist.; rented at $.50 per year for 99 years)	87
1 Nov 1839	Stephen McCorkle (on Half Mile Cr., W. side of Catawba R., York Dist.; rented at $3.00 per year for 99 years)	176
1 Nov 1839	Robert Miller (on Half Mile Cr., W. side of Catawba R., York Dist.; rented at $5.60 per year for 99 years)	186
1 Nov 1839	Thomas Sales (E. side Sugar Cr., Lancaster Dist.; rented at $3.25 per year for 99 years)	313
2 Nov 1839	James Gordon (Lancaster Dist.; formerly J. P. Winget's)	150
2 Nov 1839	Joseph Starnes (York Dist.; side lease from Sarah Starnes, originally Henry Fewell's)	112
9 Nov 1839	Thomas K. Cureton (on E. side of Sugar Cr., Lancaster Dist.; formerly Robert Robinson)	300
4 Dec 1839	J. Smith Miller (on E. side of Sugar Cr., Lancaster Dist.; formerly B. F. Davidson's)	150
6 Dec 1839	J. M. Cooper (W. side of Catawba R., York Dist.; formerly held by Joseph McCorkle, Esq.)	353 1/2
10 Dec 1839	George P. White (formerly James Miller & Samuel Roach's)	14
12 Dec 1839	E. S. Colvert (on 6 Mile Cr., Lancaster Dist.)	110
19 Dec 1839	William T. Hart (E. side of Catawba R., York Dist.; lease sold for $1524, formerly James Spratt's)	182
28 Dec 1839	Bela Sizer estate (on Cow Br., E. side of 6 Mile Cr., Lancaster Dist. & NC state line; formerly Joseph Gillespie's)	244
_____ 1839	Leroy Armstrong (E. side of Catawba R., York Dist.; purchased with a note for $227 from his mother-in-law, Ann Dillard (Pettus) Clawson Kimbrell, widow of John Kimbrell who formerly held the lease)	153
5 Nov 183-	Thomas Y. Barron (on Dutchmans Cr., W. side of Catawba R., York Dist.; formerly Daniel Shaw's)	75 1/2
20 Jan 1840	Hugh Moore (on Long Br., Lancaster Dist.; formerly William Culp's)	147
25 Jan 1840	Daniel Schooley (W. side of Catawba R., York Dist.)	7 or 8
31 Jan 1840	G. Ross Roads (on Fishing Cr., W. side of Catawba R., York Dist.; off a tract of R. P. Workman)	8
5 Feb 1840	Dr. H. Cathcart (W. side of Catawba R., York Dist.)	945
9 Feb 1840	Charles Cline (W. side of Catawba R., York Dist.; formerly William P. Hagins')	100
20 Feb 1840	Drury Morrow (on Hobs Br., Lancaster Dist.; formerly William Culp's)	150
7 Mar 1840	Bartholomew Fuller (E. side of Steele Cr. Rd., E. side of Catawba R., York Dist.; formerly Robert H. Harris & Jane Harris')	78, 86
7 Mar 1840	Robert R. Mitchell (on Thorn's Ferry Rd.; E. side of Catawba R., York Dist.; formerly Henry Harris')	121
13 Mar 1840	Proposed Treaty of Nation Ford signed at the Crossroads of Nation Ford Rd, on W. side of Catawba R., York Dist.	
24 Mar 1840	Nathaniel McCommon (on Neely's Cr., W. side of Catawba R., York Dist.; formerly Wylie Pitman's)	50 1/2
28 Mar 1840	Josina Garrison (W. side of Catawba R., York Dist.; formerly Arthur Garrison's)	95, 273
30 Mar 1840	William E. White (York Di.st.: formerly John S. Harper & A. Harper's)	87
1 Jun 1840	Andrew Creswell (on Tools Fork, waters of Fishing Cr., W. side of Catawba R., York Dist.)	232
8 Jul 1840	Agnes Carothers (formerly Eli Biggers)	96
8 Aug 1840	Philemon Shurley (on Four Mile Cr., York Dist., W. side of Catawba R., York Dist.)	8

8 Aug 1840	Philemon Shurley (on waters of Four Mile Cr., W. side of Catawba R., York Dist.: formerly Alexander Fewell's)	26
20 Aug 1840	Andrew Rea (on Long Br., waters of 6 Mile Cr., Lancaster Dist.; formerly Aaron Houston's, lease purchased for $700)	260
29 Aug 1840	Isaac Jones (W. side of Catawba R., York Dist.; formerly Jacob Jones')	78 3/4
1 Sep 1840	Marcus A. Tuttle (on Camden-Salisbury Rd near Belair Village, Lancaster Dist.; formerly John T. Hagins')	2
24 Sep 1840	Benjamin Porter (Lancaster Dist.; formerly Drury Morrow's)	100
24 Sep 1840	William Rosser (Lancaster Dist.; formerly Benjamin Porter's)	100
28 Sep 1840	L. A. Pitman (on Neely's Cr., W. side of Catawba R., York Dist.; formerly Nathaniel McCommon's)	50 1/2
13 Oct 1840	William Fuller (E. side of Catawba R., York Dist.; formerly William Partlow's)	96
26 Oct 1840	D. F. Schooley (W. side of Catawba R., York Dist.; known as Wrenn's Old Mill Place, formerly Daniel Schooley's)	5
4 Dec 1840	William A. Anthony, guardian of Aquilla Dyson (on waters of Fishing Cr., W. side of Catawba R., York Dist.; formerly Wylie Little's)	62
14 Dec 1840	John Scott (formerly Henry G. Massey's)	200
16 Dec 1840	William A.Wren (on Cain Run Br., York Dist.; formerly William Crook's)	100
_____ 1840	Isaac Jones (W. side of Catawba R., York Dist.)	78 3/4
_____ 1840	Joseph McCorkle (on Neelys Br. of Fishing Cr., W. side of Catawba R., York Dist.; formerly Daniel Davis' whose widow, Mrs. Jane B. Davis, married McCorkle)	121
_____ 1840	William Davidson (E. side of Catawba R., York Dist.; formerly Jere Alderson's, taxes paid by John Springs)	497
_____ 1840	Thomas Allen, Elias McClellan, Robert McClellan, (on Wild Cat fork of Fishing Cr., W. side of Catawba R., York Dist.; formerly John N. Henry's)	290
18 Dec 1840	S. C. Legislature confirmed the Treaty of Nation Ford, ending the leasing system	

STATE APPOINTED INDIAN COMMISSIONERS

December 15, 1808:
No. 1926. AN ACT to enable the Catawba Indians to make leases of their lands for life or lives, or terms of years; and for other purposes therein mentioned. . . .

 I. . . . .it shall and may be lawful for the Catawba Indians to grant and make to any person or persons any, lease or leases, for life or lives or term of years, of any of the lands vested in them by the laws of this State; provided, that no lease shall exceed the term of ninety-nine years, or three lives, in being.

II. . . . . That the Governor for the time being shall be authorized, and he is hereby required, to appoint five fit and proper persons to superintend the leasing of the lands of the Catawba Indians in manner aforesaid; and no lease of the lands of the Catawba Indians, hereafter to be made, whether for life or lives, or terms of years, shall be held or deemed as valid and good in law, unless the same be witnessed by a majority of the said superintendents at the time of making thereof, and signed and sealed by at least four of the head men or chiefs of the said Catawba Indians: Provided, that an annual rent be reserved as a compensation for such lease; and provided also, that no payments shall at any time be made for such lease, or any part thereof, for more than three years rent in advance; and that no payments shall be deemed and held to be valid unless the same be made conformably to this Act, and receipts therefor given by such of the chiefs of the nation as usually transact their affairs, and by a majority of the said superintendents.

III. That the said superintendents shall be commissioned for the purposes aforesaid for seven years. . . .

The following are the names of commissioners/witnesses that are found on surviving leases and surveys (an incomplete list).

1785- Charles Miller (he "kept the book"), Andrew Foster, Thomas Sprott, Nathaniel Irwin
1787- Charles Miller, William Arnold, David Turner, John Robinson, Andrew Foster, Joseph Lee, Hugh Whiteside
1788- Charles Miller, Thomas Spratt, Andrew Foster
1792- Charles Miller, Thomas Spratt, Andrew Foster, Hugh Whiteside, Nathaniel Irvin
1796- Andrew Foster, Charles Miller, Thomas Spratt, Hugh White
1801- Charles Miller, Richard Ross, John Tomlinson
1803- Charles Miller, Joseph Davie, Andrew Foster
1808- George Massey, Charles Miller, Hugh White, William Pettus
1810 - Joseph Davie, George Massey, Charles Miller, William Pettus, Hugh White.
1811- Joseph Davie, George Massey, Charles Miller, William Pettus, Hugh White
1812-William Pettus, George Massey, Hugh White, Thomas Robertson
1813-William Pettus, George Massey, Hugh White, Thomas Robertson, James M. Harris
1814-William Pettus, Thomas Robertson, Hugh White, George Massey
1815- William Pettus, Thomas Robertson, Hugh White
1816- William Pettus, Thomas Robertson, Charles Robertson, Hugh White, James M. Harris
1817- Thomas Robertson, James M. Harris, Hugh White
1818- James M. Harris, Charles Robertson, Thomas Robertson, Hugh White
1819- Benjamin Harper, Charles Robertson, Hugh White, Thomas Robertson, James M.   Harris
1820- Hugh White, Thomas Robertson, James M. Harris, Benjamin Harper
1821- Hugh White, Thomas Robertson, Charles Robertson
1822- Hugh White, James M. Harris, Charles Robertson
1823- Thomas Robertson, Benjamin Person, Benjamin Harper, Hugh White
1824- Benjamin Harper, Benjamin Person, Thomas Robertson, Hugh White
1825- William Miller
1827- William Miller, Benjamin Person, Hugh White, William White
1830- Josina Garrison, John Massey, Benjamin Persons
1831- Josina Garrison, John Massey, John L. Miller, Josina Garrison
1834- David Hagins, Joseph F. White, William White, Josina Garrison
1836- David Hagins, Joseph F. White, William White, Josina Garrison
1839- Joseph F. White, David Hagins, Josina Garrison

This is the text typically used in the appointment of new commissioners:

Resolved that Wm. F. David- Jno L. Miller, Jno Doby and Jno L. Sitgreaves be and they are hereby appointed Commissioners and invested with power & authority on the part of this State to negotiate with & to obtain from the Chiefs & Head Men of the Catawba Nation of Indians, their right & title to the land reserved for their use upon such terms as the said Commissioners or a majority of them, shall _____ expedient, provided that no compact or agreement entered into for this purpose shall be obligatory untill approved by the Legislature. And that the said Commissioners report hereon at the next session of the Legislature.

Rent Book (circa 1825) *The following records of rent money paid by lessors to Catawba Indians are taken from Hugh White's notations in Surveyor's Plat Book and Indian Commissioners Rent Book. All tenants were on the east side of the Catawba River.*

Tenant's Name	Receiver's Name	Tenant's Name	Receiver's Name
William Alderson	John Genett Brown	Matthew Marable	Col. Jacob Ayres
Churchwell Anderson	John Joe	William McWatters	Peter Harris
Esmond Acock	Gen. Jacob Scott	James Morrow	Sally Ayres
Thomas Black	Jesse Ayres	John Mills	Jesse Ayres
Saml McWhorter Billue	Jamey Kegg	Jonathan Neely	Jamey Scott
Thomas Boyd		Benjamin Patterson	Billy Ayres
Jane Baxter	Prissy Bullen	William Pettus (3)	1 Betsy Kennedy 2 Billy Canty
John Black	Jesse Ayres	William Parks	Col. Jacob Ayres
John Culp	Stephen Chitner	Benjamn Person	Jamey Brown
Simon Clymore	Betsey Kegg	William Partlow	Johnston Kennedy
Alexander Candlish	Moses Ayres	Richard Ross	Once was Billy Williams' rent
Agness Crockett	Lewis Canty	Thomas Roach	Prissy Bullen
Jeremiah Cheek	Sally Jinney's dau.	Andrew Rea	Nanny Kegg
James Darnel		James Story	Jamey Kegg
Jno Doby & Joseph Doby	Col. Jacob Ayres & $2.50 each yearly Jim Scott	John Springs	Billy Ayres $5 place; Susy Brown $2 place; Col. Jacob Ayres, $3
William Doby	Peter Harris	Alexander Scott	W. Redhead $5 place
William B. Elliott	Sally New River	Drury Smith	Jamey's daughter' the widow Gilbert George
Samuel Elliott	Sally New River	Robert Saville	Widow Redhead
Arthur Erwin	Betsy Kegg	James Spratt (4)	#3 Sally New River 1 on Steel Creek Jamey Clinton
John Gillon	Nancy Ayres	Stephen Smith	Sally New River
Isaac Garrison	Jamey Clinton	John Steel	Jamey Kegg
Joshua Gordon	Capt. Thos. Brown	John Smith	John G. Brown
Matthew Goodrich (2)	Katy Scott & Mary Scott	Jesse Sledge	Nation all
Hartwell Glover	Jamey Brown	James Spears	Stephen's children
Andrew Heron (2)	Sally New River & D. Bullen	Richard Springs (2)	Sally Scott, $10 place Jesse Ayres
John Hunter	Betsey Kegg	Joshua Tilghman	Prissy Bullen
Alexander Haynes	Katty Scott	John Thompson	Stephens daughter
George Haskett	Lewis Canty	Hez. Thorn (2)	Jamey Scott, 50 cents Sally Cantey $5 down below his house
James Harris S. Creek	W. Redhead home place; Johnston Kennedy the Carter place	Henry Talley	Sugar Jamey Give to Jamey Clinton
Nathaniel Harris	W. Redhead	Wilson Weathers	John Ayres
John Harris	W. Redhead	H. White	Sally N River
Robert Harris homeplace	Patsy Brown	Wm. White	Gen. J. Scott
Hamlin Horn	Rebecca Mursh	Martha White	Sally N River
Estate of James Webb	James Patterson	Wm E. White	Sally N River 2 1/2 dolls place, Col. Jacob Ayres the other part
John H. Hood	Jesse Ayres	David Watson	For Katy Scott 2 dolls Billy Scott
Zebb Jackson (2)	Genl Jacob Scott $5 a year & James Ayres 250 cents a year	Robert Watson	Same
William Jackson	Johnston Kennedy	James Webb	Mill place to Jacob Ayres & Katy Scott. Fishery to James Patterson
Andrew King	Susan Redhead	Isaac Weathers	Nancy Brown
Spell Kimbrell	Susan Redhead	Edmond Weathers	Same
James Moore	Prissy Bullen	John Wallace	Betsy Kennedy
Sarah McGill & John McGill	W. Redhead	Benjamin Weathers	Widow Brown
Bart. Meachem	Jamey Clinton	Estate of James Harris	Mill place Richard Kennedy
Charles Miller (2)	Prissey Bullen, 12 Mile Cr; Peter Harris Waggon Road place	John Gibbons	Thos. Brown
James Miller	Jesse Ayres	James Hutchison	Jesse Ayres
John Mills	Same		